SECOND EDITION

A Basic Guide to Importing

Compiled by
U.S. Customs Service
Department of the Treasury

NTC Business Books
a division of *NTC Publishing Group* • Lincolnwood, Illinois USA

Library of Congress Cataloging-in-Publication Data

A basic guide to importing / compiled by United States
    Customs Service.—2nd ed.

      p.   cm.
    ISBN 0-8442-3378-1
    1. Imports—United States—Handbooks, manuals,
    etc.   2. Foreign trade regulation—United States—
    Handbooks, manuals, etc. I. U.S. Customs Service.
    HF3035.B373   1993
    658.7′2—dc20   93-4389
                                        CIP

This edition first published in 1994 by
NTC Business Books, a division of
NTC Publishing Group, 4255 West Touhy Avenue,
Lincolnwood (Chicago), Illinois 60646-1975 U.S.A.,
is an unabridged publication of *Importing into the United States,*
revised second edition, compiled by the United States Customs
Service, 1991.
Manufactured in the United States of America.

3 4 5 6 7 8 9 0 VP 9 8 7 6 5 4 3 2 1

contents

CUSTOMS ORGANIZATION 1 Organization: Ports of Entry 1
Suggestions to the Exporter 6

ENTRY OF GOODS 2 Entry Process 7
3 Right to Make Entry 9
4 Examination of Goods 11
5 Packing—Commingling 13

INVOICES 6 Commercial Invoice 15
7 Other Invoices 16
8 Frequent Errors in Invoicing 17

ASSESSMENT OF DUTY 9 Dutiable Status of Goods 18
10 Containers or Holders 19
11 Temporary Free Importations 20
12 U.S./Canada Free Trade Agreement (FTA) 22
13 Generalized System of Preferences 23
14 Caribbean Basin Initiative 26
15 U.S.-Israel Free Trade Area Agreement 27
16 Compact of Free Association (FAS) 29
17 Antidumping and Countervailing Duties 29
18 Drawback—Refund of Duties 30

CLASSIFICATION 19 Classification—Liquidation 32
AND VALUE 20 Conversion of Currency 33
21 Transaction Value 33
22 Transaction Value—Similar or Identical Merchandise 36
23 Other Bases: Deductive and Computed Value 37

MARKING 24 Country of Origin Marking 41
25 Special Marking Requirements 43
26 Marking—False Impression 44
27 User Fees 45

SPECIAL REQUIREMENTS 28 Prohibitions, Restrictions, and Other Agency Requirements . . . 46
29 Alcoholic Beverages 55
30 Motor Vehicles and Boats 56
31 Import Quotas 57

FRAUD 32 Civil and Criminal Fraud Laws 60

FOREIGN-TRADE ZONES 33 Foreign-Trade Zones 61

APPENDIX 65

foreword

The volume, variety, and complexity of commodities entering the United States each year require that certain importing procedures be followed. These procedures, outlined in this book, help assure that imports are processed as accurately and quickly as possible. They also help protect American business in international trade. Some of these requirements must be met by foreign exporters, whose cooperation in such things as invoice preparation and marking, for example, is critical if American importers of their merchandise are to comply with U.S. Customs requirements.

Business people abroad who need accurate information about Customs matters not covered here may contact a U.S. Customs attaché or representative at the nearest American consulate. They may also call or write to a Customs official in the United States or write to the District Director of Customs at any of the district ports listed in Chapter One (Customs Organization) or to the Commissioner of Customs.

We have made every effort to include the essential importing requirements, but it is not possible for a book this size to cover all Customs laws and regulations. Importers should also be aware that this book does not supersede or modify any provision of those laws and regulations. Legislative and administrative changes are always under consideration; such changes can occur at any time. Similarly, quota limitations on commodities are also subject to change. Foreign exporters and American importers are advised to keep abreast of quotas applicable to their merchandise.

If you are a commercial importer or anticipate becoming one, we urge you to stay in contact with your nearest Custom district office for changes in any of the requirements described in this book. Customs offices not listed here can be found in your local telephone directory under the Department of the Treasury.

CAROL HALLETT,
Commissioner of Customs.

1 customs organization

Mission

The major responsibility of the U.S. Customs Service is to administer the Tariff Act of 1930, as amended. Primary duties include the assessment and collection of all duties, taxes, and fees on imported merchandise, the enforcement of customs and related laws, and the administration of certain navigation laws and treaties. As a major enforcement organization, the Customs Service combats smuggling and frauds on the revenue and enforces the regulations of numerous other Federal agencies at ports of entry and along the land and sea borders of the United States.

Organization

The customs territory of the United States consists of the 50 states, the District of Columbia, and Puerto Rico. The Customs Service, an agency under the Department of the Treasury, has its headquarters in Washington, D.C., and is headed by a Commissioner of Customs. The field organization consists of seven geographical regions further divided into districts with ports of entry within each district. These organizational elements are headed respectively by regional commissioners, district directors (or area directors in the case of the New York region), and port directors. The Customs Service is also responsible for administering the customs laws of the Virgin Islands of the United States.

Both an alphabetical list of all ports by State and a list of districts by region (including postal ZIP code) are provided. Whenever it is suggested that you write to the district or port director for information, the director referred to is the one at the district or port where your goods will be entered.

Ports of Entry by State
(Including Puerto Rico and the U.S. Virgin Islands)

Key:
Districts shown in boldface
• Regional Headquarters
* Consolidated ports

ALABAMA
Birmingham
Huntsville
Mobile

ALASKA
Alcan
Anchorage
Dalton Cache
Fairbanks
Juneau
Ketchikan
Sitka
Skagway
Valdez
Wrangell

ARIZONA
Douglas
Lukeville
Naco
Nogales
Phoenix
San Luis
Sasabe

ARKANSAS
Little Rock-N. Little Rock

CALIFORNIA
Andrade
Calexico
Eureka
Fresno
• **Los Angeles-Long Beach**
Port San Luis
San Diego
San Francisco-Oakland
Tecate
San Ysidro

COLORADO
Denver

CONNECTICUT
Bridgeport
Hartford

New Haven
New London

DELAWARE
Wilmington
(See Philadelphia)

DISTRICT OF COLUMBIA
Washington

FLORIDA
Apalachicola
Boca Grande
Carrabelle
Fernandina Beach
Jacksonville
Key West
• **Miami**
Orlando
Panama City
Pensacola
Port Canaveral
Port Everglades
Port St. Joe
St. Petersburg
Tampa
West Palm Beach
Port Manatee

GEORGIA
Atlanta
Brunswick
Savannah

HAWAII
Honolulu
Hilo
Kahului
Nawiliwili-Port Allen

IDAHO
Eastport
Porthill
Boise

ILLINOIS
• Chicago
Peoria
Rock Island-Moline*
(See Davenport)

INDIANA
Evansville/Owens-
boro, Ky.
Indianapolis
Lawrenceburg/Cin-
cinnati, Ohio

IOWA
Davenport-Rock
Island-Moline*
Des Moines

KANSAS
Wichita

KENTUCKY
Louisville
Owensboro/Evans-
ville, Ind.

LOUISIANA
Baton Rouge
Gramercy
Lake Charles
Morgan City
• **New Orleans**
Shreveport/Bossier
City

MAINE
Bangor
Bar Harbor
Bath
Belfast
Bridgewater
Calais
Eastport
Fort Fairfield
Fort Kent
Houlton

Jackman
Jonesport
Limestone
Madawaska
Portland
Rockland
Van Buren
Vanceboro

MARYLAND
Annapolis
Baltimore
Cambridge

MASSACHUSETTS
• **Boston**
Fall River
Gloucester
Lawrence
New Bedford
Plymouth
Salem
Springfield
Worcester

MICHIGAN
Battle Creek
Detroit
Grand Rapids
Muskegon
Port Huron
Saginaw-Bay City/Flint
Sault Ste. Marie

MINNESOTA
Baudette
Duluth and Superior, Wis.
Grand Portage
International Falls-Ranier
Minneapolis-St. Paul
Noyes
Pinecreek
Roseau
Warroad

MISSISSIPPI
Greenville
Gulfport
Pascagoula
Vicksburg

MISSOURI
Kansas City
St. Joseph
St. Louis
Springfield
  (Temporary)

MONTANA
Butte
Del Bonita
Great Falls
Morgan
Opheim
Piegan
Raymond
Roosville
Scobey
Sweetgrass
Turner
Whitetail
Whitlash

NEBRASKA
Omaha

NEVADA
Las Vegas
Reno

NEW HAMPSHIRE
Portsmouth

NEW JERSEY
Perth Amboy (See
New York/Newark)

NEW MEXICO
Albuquerque
Columbus

NEW YORK
Albany
Alexandria Bay
Buffalo-Niagara Falls
Cape Vincent
Champlain-Rouses Point
Chateaugay
Clayton
Fort Covington
Massena
• New York
  Kennedy Airport Area
  Newark Area
  New York Seaport Area

Ogdensburg
Oswego
Rochester
Sodus Point
Syracuse
Trout River
Utica

NORTH CAROLINA
Beaufort-Morehead City
Charlotte
Durham
Reidsville
Wilmington
Winston-Salem

NORTH DAKOTA
Ambrose
Antler
Carbury
Dunseith
Fortuna
Hannah
Hansboro
Maida
Neche
Noonan
Northgate
Pembina
Portal
Sarles
Sherwood
St. John
Walhalla
Westhope

OHIO
Akron
Ashtabula/Conneaut
Cincinnati/Lawrence-
burg, Ind.
Cleveland
Columbus
Dayton
Toledo/Sandusky

OKLAHOMA
Oklahoma City
Tulsa

OREGON
Coos Bay
Newport
Portland*

PENNSYLVANIA
Chester (See Phila.)
Erie
Harrisburg

**Philadelphia/Chester/
Wilmington**
Pittsburgh
Wilkes-Barre/Scranton

PUERTO RICO
Aguadilla
Fajardo
Guanica
Humacao
Jobos
Mayaguez
Ponce
San Juan

RHODE ISLAND
Newport
Providence

SOUTH CAROLINA
Charleston
Georgetown
Greenville-Spartanburg

TENNESSEE
Chattanooga
Knoxville
Memphis
Nashville

TEXAS
Amarillo
Austin
Beaumont*
Brownsville
Corpus Christi
Dallas/Ft. Worth
Del Rio
Eagle Pass
El Paso
Fabens
Freeport
Hidalgo
• Houston/Galveston
Laredo
Lubbock
Orange*
Port Arthur*
Port Lavaca-Point Comfort
Presidio
Progreso
Rio Grande City
Roma
Sabine*
San Antonio

UTAH
Salt Lake City

VERMONT
Beecher Falls

Burlington
Derby Line
Highgate Springs/Alburg
Norton
Richford
St. Albans

VIRGIN ISLANDS
**Charlotte Amalie,
  St. Thomas**
Christiansted
Coral Bay
Cruz Bay
Frederiksted

VIRGINIA
Alexandria
Cape Charles City
Norfolk-Newport News
Reedville
Richmond-Petersburg

WASHINGTON
Aberdeen
Anacortes*
Bellingham*
Blaine
Boundary
Danville
Everett*
Ferry
Friday Harbor*
Frontier
Laurier
Longview*
Lynden
Metaline Falls
Neah Bay*
Nighthawk
Olympia*
Oroville
Point Roberts
Port Angeles*
Port Townsend*
Seattle*
Spokane
Sumas
Tacoma*

WEST VIRGINIA
Charleston

WISCONSIN
Ashland
Green Bay
Manitowoc
Marinette
Milwaukee
Racine
Sheboygan

* Consolidated Ports:
  Columbia River port of entry includes Longview, Washington, and Pordand, OR.
  Beaumont, Orange, Port Arthur, Sabine port of entry includes ports of the same name.
  Port of Puget Sound includes Tacoma, Seattle, Port Angeles, Port Townsend, Neah Bay, Friday Harbor, Everette, Bellingham, Anacortes,
  and Olympia in the State of Washington.
  Port of Philadelphia includes Wilmington and Chester.
  Port of Rock Island includes Moline and Davenport, IA.
  Port of Shreveport includes Bossier City, LA.
Designated User-fee Airports: Allentown-Bethlehem-Easton, PA; Casper, WY; Columbus, OH; Dona Ana County, NM; Fargo, ND; Ft.
Myers, FL; Ft. Wayne, IN; Jackson, MS; Klamath County, OR; Lebanon, NH; Lexington, KY; Midland, TX; Morristown, NJ; Oakland-
Pontiac, MI; Rockford, IL; Sanford, FL; St. Paul, AK; Waukegan, IL; Wilmington, OH; Yakima, WA.

Customs Regions and Districts

Headquarters
U.S. Customs Service
1301 Constitution Ave., N.W.
Washington, D.C. 20229

**Northeast Region—
Boston, Mass. 02222-1056**
Districts:
Portland, Maine 04112
St. Albans, Vt. 05478
Boston, Mass. 02222-1056
Providence, R.I. 02905
Buffalo, N.Y. 14202
Ogdensburg, N.Y. 13669
Philadelphia, Pa. 19106
Baltimore, Md. 21202
Norfolk, Va. 23510
Washington, D.C. 20041

**New York Region—
New York, N.Y. 10048**
New York Seaport Area
New York, N.Y. 10048
Kennedy Airport Area
Jamaica, N.Y. 11430
Newark Area
Newark, N.J. 07102

**Southeast Region—
Miami, Fla. 33131**
Districts:
Wilmington, N.C. 28401
San Juan, P.R. 00901
Charleston, S.C. 29402
Savannah, Ga. 31401
Tampa Fla. 33605
Miami Fla. 33131
St. Thomas, V.I. 00801

**South Central Region—
New Orleans, La. 70130**
Districts:
Mobile, Ala. 36602
New Orleans, La. 70130

**Southwest Region—
Houston, Tex. 77057**
Districts:
Port Arthur, Tex. 77642
Houston/Galveston, Tex. 77029
Laredo, Tex. 78041-3130
El Paso, Tex. 79985
Dallas/Fort Worth, Tex. 75261

**Pacific Region—
Los Angeles, Calif. 90831-0700**
Districts:
Nogales, Ariz. 85621
San Diego, Calif. 92188
Los Angeles/Long Beach,
Calif. 90731
San Francisco, Calif. 94126
Honolulu, Hawaii 96806
Portland, Ore. 97209
Seattle, Wash. 98104
Anchorage, Alaska 99501
Great Falls, Mont. 59405

**North Central Region—
Chicago, Ill. 60603-5790**
Districts:
Chicago, Ill. 60607
Pembina, N.D. 58271
Minneapolis-St. Paul, Minn.
55401
Duluth, Minn. 55802-1390
Milwaukee, Wis. 53237-0260
Cleveland, Ohio 44114
St. Louis, Mo. 63105
Detroit, Mich. 48226-2568

U.S. Custom Officers in Foreign Countries

Austria
Customs Attaché
American Embassy
Boltzmanngasse 16, A-1091
Vienna
Tel: 315–5511 Ext. 2112

Belgium
Customs Attaché
U.S. Mission to the European
Communities
PSC 82 Box 002
APO AE 09724
Tel: 502–3300

Canada
Customs Attaché
American Embassy
100 Wellington St.
Ottawa, Ontario
Canada, KIP 5TI
Tel: (613) 238–5335 Ext. 322

France
Customs Attaché
American Embassy
58 bis Rue la Boetie
Room 3 17
76008 Paris
Tel: 4296–1202 Ext. 2392/2393

Hong Kong, B.C.C.
Senior Customs Representative
American Consulate General
St. John's Building-11th Floor
33 Garden Road
Tel: 5-239011 Ext. 244

Italy
Customs Attaché
American Embassy
Via Veneto 119
Rome, Italy
Tel: 6-467-42475

Senior Customs Representative
American Consulate General
Via Principe Amedeo
2/10-20121 Milano
Tel: 2–655–4973

Japan
Customs Attaché
American Embassy
10-5 Akasaka l-Chome
Minato-ku, Tokyo 107
Japan
Tel: 81–3–3224–5433

Korea
Customs Attaché
82 SeJong Ro
Chongro-Ku
Seoul 110-050
Tel: 732–2601, Ext. 4563

Mexico
Customs Attaché
American Embassy
Paseo De La Reforma 305
Colonia Cuahtemoc
Mexico City, Mexico
Tel: 211–042, Ext. 3687

Sr. Customs Representative
American Consulate General
No. 139 Morelia
Hermosillo Son., Mexico
Tel: 621–7–5258

Sr. Customs Representative
American Consulate
Paseo Montejo 453
Merida, Yucatan
Mexico 97000
Tel: 99–25–8235

Sr. Customs Representative
American Consulate General
Avenida Constitucion
411 Poniente
Monterrey N.L., Mexico
Tel: 45–21–20

The Netherlands
Customs Attaché
American Embassy
Lange Voorhout 102
2514EJ The Hague, Netherlands
Tel: 703–924–651

Panama
Customs Attaché
Calle 38 & Avenida Balboa
Panama, R.P.
Tel: 507271777, Ext. 2440

Singapore
Customs Attaché
American Embassy
30 Hill Road
Singapore 0617
Tel: 621–7–5258

Thailand
Customs Attaché
American Embassy
95 Wireless Road
Bangkok
Tel: 252-5040 Ext. 2539

United Kingdom
Customs Attaché
American Embassy
24/31 Grosvenor Square
London, W. 1A 1AE
Tel: 71/493–4599

Uruguay
Customs Attaché
American Embassy
APO Miami, FL 34035
Tel: 598–223–6061

West Germany
Customs Attaché
American Embassy
Deichmanns Aue. 29
5300 Bonn 2
Tel: 228/3392207
228/3312853

3

EASTERN

NORTHEAST

SOUTHEAST

SOUTH CENTRAL

NORTH CENTRAL

LEGEND

- • PORT OF ENTRY
- ⋆ DISTRICT OFFICE (also Port of Entry)
- ★ REGIONAL HEADQUARTERS (also district office and Port of Entry)
- ---- STATE BOUNDARY
- —— DISTRICT BOUNDARY
- ▪▪▪ REGIONAL BOUNDARY
- ¦¦¦ TIME ZONE
- ■ User Fee Airports

PRECLEARANCE STATIONS

NORTH CENTRAL REGION
Montreal
Toronto
Winnipeg
Calgary
Edmonton
Vancouver

SOUTHEAST REGION
Bermuda
Freeport
Nassau

REVISED 9/91

PUERTO RICO - VIRGIN I.

FAJARDO
AGUADILLA
SAN JUAN
MAYAGUEZ
GUANICA
JOBOS
PONCE
HUMACAO
CHARLOTTE
AMALIE
CRUZ BAY
CORAL BAY
CHRISTIANSTED
FREDERIKSTED

Included in Southeast

suggestions to the exporter

FOR FASTER CUSTOMS CLEARANCE:

1 Include all information required on your customs invoices.

2 Prepare your invoices carefully. Type them clearly. Allow sufficient space between lines. Keep the data within each column.

3 Make sure that your invoices contain the information that would be shown on a well-prepared packing list.

4 Mark and number each package so that it can be identified with the corresponding marks and numbers appearing on your invoice.

5 Show on your invoice a detailed description of each item of goods contained in each individual package.

6 Mark your goods legibly and conspicuously with the name of the country of origin, unless they are specifically exempted from the country of origin marking requirements, and with such other marking as required by the marking laws of the United States. Exemptions and general marking requirements are detailed in Chapters 24 and 25.

7 Comply with the provisions of any special laws of the United States which may apply to your goods, such as the laws relating to foods, drugs, cosmetics, alcoholic beverages, and radioactive materials.

8 Observe closely the instructions with respect to invoicing, packaging, marking, labeling, etc., sent you by your customer in the United States. He has probably made a careful check of the requirements which will have to be met when you arrive.

9 Work with U.S. Customs in developing packing standards for your commodities.

10 Establish sound security procedures at your facility and while transporting your goods for shipment. Do not allow narcotic smugglers the opportunity to introduce narcotics into your shipment.

2   entry process

When a shipment reaches the United States, the consignee will file entry documents for the goods with the district or port director at the port of entry. Imported goods are not legally entered until after the shipment has arrived within the port of entry, delivery of the merchandise has been authorized by Customs and estimated duties have been paid. It is the responsibility of the importer to arrange for examination and release of the goods.

NOTE: In addition to the U.S. Customs Service, importers should contact other agencies when questions regarding particular commodities arise. For example, questions about products regulated by the Food and Drug Administration should be forwarded to the nearest FDA district office (check local phone book under "U.S. Government" listings) or to the Import Division, FDA Headquarters, (301) 443-6553. The same is true for alcohol, tobacco, firearms, wildlife products (furs, skins, shells), motor vehicles, and other products and merchandise regulated by the 60 federal agencies for which Customs enforces entry laws. Appropriate agencies are identified elsewhere in this book.

Goods may be entered for consumption, entered for warehouse at the port of arrival, or they may be transported in-bond to another port of entry and entered there under the same conditions as at the port of arrival. Arrangements for transporting the merchandise to an interior port in-bond may be made by the consignee, by a customs broker, or by any other person having a sufficient interest in the goods for that purpose. *Unless your merchandise arrives directly at the port where you wish to enter it, you may be charged additional fees by the carriers for transportation to that port if other arrangements have not been made.* Under some circumstances, your goods may be released through your local Customs port even though they arrive at another port from a foreign country. Arrangements must be made prior to arrival at the Customs port where you intend to file your duties and documentation.

Goods to be placed in a foreign-trade zone are not entered at the customhouse. See Chapter 33 for further information.

Evidence of Right to Make Entry

Goods may be entered only by the owner, purchaser, or a licensed customhouse broker. When the goods are consigned "to order," the bill of lading properly endorsed by the consignor may serve as evidence of the right to make entry. An airway bill may be used for merchandise arriving by air.

In most instances, entry is made by a person or firm certified by the carrier bringing the goods to the port of entry and is considered the "owner" of the goods for customs purposes. The document issued by the carrier is known as a "Carrier's Certificate." An example of the format is shown in the appendix. In certain circumstances, entry may be made by means of a duplicate bill of lading or a shipping receipt.

Entry for Consumption

The entry of merchandise is a two-part process consisting of (1) filing the documents necessary to determine whether merchandise may be released from Customs custody and (2) filing the documents which contain information for duty assessment and statistical purposes. In certain instances, such as the entry of merchandise subject to quotas, all documents must be filed and accepted by Customs prior to the release of the goods.

Entry Documents

Within five working days of the date of arrival of a shipment at a U.S. port of entry, entry documents must be filed at a location specified by the district/area director, unless an extension is granted. These documents consist of:

a. Entry Manifest, Customs Form 7533; or Application and Special Permit for Immediate Delivery, Customs Form 3461, or other form of merchandise release required by the district director.

b. Evidence of right to make entry.

c. Commercial invoice or a pro forma invoice when the commercial invoice cannot be produced.

d. Packing lists if appropriate.

e. Other documents necessary to determine merchandise admissibility.

If the goods are to be released from Customs custody on entry documents, an entry summary for consumption must be filed and estimated duties deposited at the port of entry within 10 working days of the time the goods are entered and released.

Surety

The entry must be accompanied by evidence that a bond is posted with Customs to cover any potential duties, taxes, and penalties which may accrue. Bonds may be secured through a resident U.S. surety company but may be posted in the form of United States money or certain United States government obligations. In the event that a customhouse broker is employed for the purpose of making entry, the broker may permit the use of his bond to provide the required coverage.

Entry Summary Documentation

Following presentation of the entry, the shipment may be examined or examination may be waived. The shipment is then released, provided no legal or regulatory violations have occurred. Entry summary documentation is filed and estimated duties are deposited within 10 working days of the release of the merchandise at a designated customhouse. Entry summary documentation consists of:

a. The entry package returned to the importer, broker, or his authorized agent after merchandise is permitted release.

b. Entry summary (Customs Form 7501)

c. Other invoices and documents necessary for the assessment of duties, collection of statistics, or the determination that all import requirements have been satisfied.

Immediate Delivery

An alternate procedure which provides for immediate release of a shipment may be used in some cases by making application for a Special Permit for Immediate Delivery on Customs Form 3461 prior to the arrival of the merchandise. If the application is approved, the shipment is released expeditiously following arrival. An entry summary must then be filed in proper form and estimated duties deposited within 10 working days of release. Release using Form 3461 is limited to the following merchandise:

a. Merchandise arriving from Canada or Mexico, if approved by the district director and an appropriate bond is on file.

b. Fresh fruits and vegetables for human consumption arriving from Canada and Mexico and removed from the area immediately contiguous to the border to the importer's premises within the port of importation.

c. Shipments consigned to or for the account of any agency or officer of the U.S. Government.

d. Articles for a trade fair.

e. Tariff-rate quota merchandise and under certain circumstances merchandise subject to an absolute quota. Absolute quota items require a formal entry at all times.

f. In very limited circumstances, merchandise released from warehouse followed within 10 working days by a warehouse withdrawal for consumption.

g. Merchandise specifically authorized by Customs Headquarters to be entitled to release for immediate delivery.

Entry for Warehouse

If it is desired to postpone the release of the goods, they may be placed in a Customs bonded warehouse under a warehouse entry. The goods may remain in the bonded warehouse up to five years from the date of importation. At any time during that period, warehoused goods may be reexported without the payment of duty or they may be withdrawn for consumption upon the payment of duty at the rate of duty in effect on the date of withdrawal. If the goods are destroyed under Customs supervision, no duty is payable.

While the goods are in the bonded warehouse, they may, under Customs supervision, be manipulated by cleaning, sorting, repacking, or otherwise changing their condition by processes which do not amount to manufacturing. After manipulation and within the warehousing period, the goods may be exported without the payment of duty or they may be withdrawn for consumption upon payment of duty at the rate applicable to the goods in their manipulated condition at the time of withdrawal. Perishable goods, explosive substances, or prohibited importations may not be placed in a bonded warehouse. Certain restricted articles, though not allowed release from custody, may be warehoused.

Information regarding bonded manufacturing warehouses is contained in section 311 of the Tariff Act. (19 U.S.C. 1311).

Unentered Goods

If there is a failure to file an entry for the goods at the port of entry or port of destination for in-bond shipments within five working days after arrival, the district or port director may place them in a general order warehouse at the risk and expense of the importer. If the goods are not entered within one year from the date of importation, they can be sold at public auction. Perishable goods, goods liable to depreciation, and explosive substances, however, may be sold sooner.

Storage charges, expenses of sale, internal revenue taxes, duties and amounts for the satisfaction of liens must be taken out of the money obtained from the sale of the unentered goods. Any surplus remaining after these deductions is ordinarily payable to the holder of a duly endorsed bill of lading covering the goods. If the goods are subject to internal revenue taxes and will not bring enough on sale at public auction to pay the taxes, they are subject to destruction.

Mail Entries

Importers have found that in some cases it is to their advantage to use the mails to import merchandise into the United States. Some benefits to be gained are:

a. Ease in clearing shipments through Customs. The duties on parcels valued at $1,250 or less are collected by the letter carrier delivering the parcel to the addressee (see note below).

b. Savings on shipping charges. Smaller, low-valued packages can often be sent less expensively through the mails.

c. No entry required on duty-free merchandise not exceeding $1,250 in value.

d. No need to clear shipments personally if under $1,250 in value.

Joint Customs and postal regulations provide that all parcel post packages must have a Customs declaration securely attached giving an accurate description and the value of the contents. This declaration is obtained at post offices. Commercial shipments must also be accompanied by a commercial invoice enclosed in the parcel bearing the declaration.

Each mail article containing an invoice or statement of value should be marked on the address side "Invoice enclosed." If the invoice or statement cannot conveniently be enclosed within the sealed article, it may be securely attached to the article. Failure to comply with any of these requirements will delay clearance of the shipment through Customs.

Packages other than parcel post, such as letter-class mail, commercial papers, printed matter, and samples of merchandise, must bear on the address side a label, Form C1, provided by the Universal Postal Union, or the endorsement "May be opened for customs purposes before delivery" or similar words definitely waiving the privacy of the seal and indicating that Customs officers may open the parcel without recourse to the addressee. Parcels not labeled or endorsed in this manner and found to contain merchandise subject to duty or tax are subject to forfeiture.

A Customs officer prepares the customs entry for mail importations not exceeding $1,250 in value, and the letter carrier at the destination delivers the parcel to the addressee upon payment of the duty. If the value of a mail importation exceeds $1,250, the addressee is notified to prepare and file a formal Customs entry (consumption entry) for it at the Customs port nearest to him. A commercial invoice is required with the entry.

A Customs processing fee of $5.00 will be assessed on each item of dutiable mail for which a Customs officer prepares documentation. A nominal charge on all dutiable or taxable mail, in addition to the duty, is collected from the addressee. There is also a postal fee (in addition to prepaid postage) authorized by international postal conventions and agreements as partial reimbursement to the Postal Service for its work in clearing packages through Customs and delivering them.

Note: The following general exceptions apply to the $1,250 limit:

Articles classified in sub-chapters III and IV, chapter 99, HTSUS	Leather, articles of
Billfolds and other flat goods	Luggage
Feathers and feather products	Millinery ornaments
Flowers and foliage, artificial or preserved	Pillows and cushions
Footwear	Plastics, miscellaneous articles of
Fur, articles of	Rawhides and skins
Gloves	Rubber, miscellaneous articles of
Handbags	Textile fibers and products
Headwear and hat braids	Toys, games, and sports equipment
	Trimmings

The limit for these articles is set at $250. Unaccompanied shipments of made-to-measure suits from Hong Kong require a formal entry regardless of value.

3 right to make entry

Entry by Importer

Merchandise arriving in the United States by commercial carrier must be entered by the owner, purchaser, his authorized regular employee, or by the owner's licensed Customs broker. U.S. Customs officers and employees are not authorized to act as agents for importers or forwarders of imported merchandise, although they may give all reasonable advice and assistance to inexperienced importers.

The only persons who are authorized by the tariff laws of the United States to act as agents for importers in the transaction of their Customs business are Customs brokers who are private individuals or firms licensed by the Customs Service. Customs brokers will prepare and file the necessary Customs entries arrange for the payment of the duties found due, take steps to effect the release of the goods in Customs custody, and otherwise represent their principals in customs matters. The fees charged for these services may vary according to the Customs broker and the extent of services performed.

Every entry must be supported by one of the forms of evidence of the right to make entry outlined in this chapter. When entry is made by a Customs broker, a Customs power of attorney given by the person or firm for whom the Customs broker is acting as agent is made in the name of the Customs broker. Ordinarily, the authority of an employee to make entry for his employer is most satisfactorily established by a Customs power of attorney.

Entries Made by Others

Entry of goods may be made by a nonresident individual or partnership, or a foreign corporation through an agent or representative of the exporter in the United States, a member of the partnership, or an officer of the corporation.

The surety on any Customs bond required from a nonresident individual or organization must be incorporated in the United States. In addition, a foreign corporation in whose name merchandise is entered must have a resident agent authorized to accept service of process in its behalf in the state where the port of entry is located.

A licensed Customs broker named in a Customs power of attorney may make entry on behalf of the exporter or his representative. The owner's declaration made by a nonresident individual or organization which the Customs broker may request must be supported by a surety bond providing for the payment of an increased or additional duties found due. Liability for duties is discussed in Chapter 9. An owner's declaration executed in a foreign country is acceptable, but it must be executed before a notary public and bear the notary's seal. Notaries public will be found in all American embassies around the world and in most of the larger consulates.

Power of Attorney

A nonresident individual, partnership, or foreign corporation may issue a power of attorney to a regular employee, Customs broker, partner, or corporation officer to transact customs business in the United States. Any person named in a power of attorney must be a resident of the United States who has been authorized to accept service of process on behalf of the person or organization issuing the power of attorney. Either the applicable Customs form (see appendix) or a document using the same language as the form is acceptable References to those acts which the issuer has not authorized his agent to perform may be deleted from the form or omitted from the document.

A power of attorney from a foreign corporation must be supported by the following documents or their equivalent when foreign law or practice differs from that in the United States:

1. A certificate from the proper public officer of the country showing the legal existence of the corporation, unless the fact of incorporation is so generally known as to be a matter of common knowledge.

2. A copy of that part of the charter or articles of incorporation which shows the scope of business of the corporation and its governing body.

3. A copy of the document or part thereof by which the person signing the power of attorney derives his authority, such as a provision of the charter or articles of incorporation, a copy of the resolution, minutes of the meeting of the board of directors or other document by which the governing body conferred the authority. In this case a copy of the bylaws or other document giving the governing board the authority to designate others to appoint agents or attorney is required.

A nonresident individual or partnership or a foreign corporation may issue a power of attorney to authorize the persons or firms named in the power of attorney to issue like powers of attorney to other qualified residents of the United States and to empower the residents to whom such powers of attorney are issued to accept service of process on behalf of the nonresident individual or organization.

A power of attorney issued by a partnership must be limited to a period not to exceed two years from the date of execution and shall state the names of all members of the partnership. One member of a partnership may execute a power of attorney for the transaction of the customs business of the partnership. When a new firm is formed by a change of membership, the power of attorney of the prior firm is no longer effective for any customs purpose. The new firm will be required to issue a power of attorney for the transaction of its custom business. All other powers of attorney may be granted for an unlimited period.

Customs Form 5291 or a document using the same language as the form is also used to empower an agent other than an attorney-at-law or Customs broker to file protests on behalf of an importer under section 514 of the Tariff Act of 1930 as amended. (See 19 CFR 141.32.)

Foreign corporations may comply with Customs regulations by executing a power of attorney on the letterhead of the corporation. A form of power of attorney used for this purpose is given below. A nonresident individual or partner may use this same form.

The X Corporation, _____
(Address, city, and country)

organized under the laws of _____ hereby authorizes

_____
(Name or names of employee or officer in United States

_____
and address or addresses)

to perform on behalf of the said corporation any and all acts specified in Customs Form 5291, Power of Attorney: to accept service of process in the United States on behalf of the X Corporation; to issue powers of attorney on Customs Form 5291 authorizing a qualified resident or residents of the United States to perform on behalf of the X Corporation all acts specified in Customs Form 5291; and to empower such resident or residents to accept service of process in the United States on behalf of the said X Corporation.

Because the laws regarding incorporation, notation, and authentication of documents vary from country to country, the agent to be named in the power of attorney should consult the district director of Customs at the port of entry where proof of the document's existence may be required as to the proper form to be used and the formalities to be met.

4 examination of goods

Prior to release of the goods, the district or port director will designate representative quantities for examination by Customs officers under conditions properly safeguarding the goods. Examination is necessary to determine:

a. The value of the goods for Customs purposes and their dutiable status.

b. Whether the goods must be marked with the country of their origin or require special marking or labeling. If so, whether they are marked in the manner required.

c. Whether the shipment contains prohibited articles.

d. Whether the goods are correctly invoiced.

e. Whether the goods are in excess of the invoiced quantities or a shortage exists.

Some kinds of goods must be examined to determine whether they meet special requirements of the law. For example, food and beverages unfit for human consumption would not meet the requirements of the Food and Drug Administration.

    f. Whether the shipment contains illegal narcotics.

One of the primary methods of smuggling narcotics into the United States is in cargo shipments. Drug smugglers will place narcotics into a legitimate cargo shipment or container to be retrieved upon arrival in the United States. Because smugglers use any means possible to hide narcotics, all aspects of the shipment are examined, including: container, pallets, boxes, and product. Only through intensive inspection can narcotics be discovered.

Textiles and textile products are considered trade-sensitive and as such may be subject to a higher percentage of examinations than other commodities.

Customs officers will ascertain the quantity of goods imported, making allowance for shortages under specified conditions and assessing duty on any excess. Certain goods will be weighed, gauged, or measured. If the invoice or entry does not state the weight, quantity, or measure of the goods, the expense of determining this data may be collected for the consignee before the goods are released from Customs custody. The invoice may state the quantities in the weights and measures of the country from which the goods are shipped or in the weights and measures of the United States, but the entry must state the quantities in metric terms.

Excess Goods and Shortages

The showing of the contents of each package on the invoice, the orderly packing of the goods, the proper marking and numbering of the packages in which the goods are packed, and the placing of the corresponding marks and numbers on the invoice facilitate the allowance in duties for goods which do not arrive and the ascertainment of whether any excess goods are contained in the shipment.

If any package which has been designated for examination is found by the Customs officer to contain any article not specified in the invoice, and there is reason to believe the article was omitted from the invoice with fraudulent intent on the part of the seller, shipper, owner, or agent, the contents of the entire package in which the excess goods are found are subject to seizure and possible forfeiture. On the other hand, when no fraudulent intent is apparent, penalties do not accrue, but the duties due, if any, will be collected on the excess goods.

When a deficiency in quantity, weight, or measure is found by the Customs officer in the examination of any package which has been dated for examination, an allowance in duty will be made for the deficiency. Allowance in duty is made for deficiencies in packages not designated for examination, provided that before liquidation of the entry becomes final, the importer notifies the district or port director of Customs of the shortage and establishes to the satisfaction of the district or port director that the missing goods were not delivered to him.

Damage or Deterioration

Goods which are found by the Customs officer to be entirely without commercial value at the time of arrival in the United States because of damage or deterioration are treated as a "nonimportation." No duties are assessed on these goods. When damage or deterioration is present with respect to part of the shipment only, allowance in duties is not made unless the importer segregates the damaged or deteriorated part from the remainder of the shipment under Customs supervision.

When the shipment consists of fruits, vegetables, or other perishable merchandise, allowance in duties cannot be made unless the importer, within 96 hours after the unlading of the merchandise and before it has been removed from Customs custody, files an application for an allowance with the district or port director.

On shipments consisting of any article partly or wholly manufactured of iron or steel, or any manufacture of iron or steel, allowance or reduction of duty for partial damage or loss as a result of discoloration or rust is precluded by law.

Tare and Draft

In ascertaining the quantity of goods dutiable on net weight, a deduction is made from the gross weight for just and reasonable tare. The following schedule tares are provided for in the Customs Regulations:

Apple boxes. 3.6 kilograms (8 lb.) per box. This schedule tare includes the paper wrappers, if any, on the apples.

China clay in so called half-ton casks. 32.6 kilograms (72 lb.) per cask.

Figs in skeleton cases. Actual tare for outer containers plus 13 percent of the gross weight of the inside wooden boxes and figs.

Fresh tomatoes. 113 grams (4 oz.) per 100 paper wrappings.

Lemons and oranges. 283 grams (10 oz.) per box and 142 grams (5 oz.) per half-box for paper wrappings, and actual tare for outer containers.

Ocher, dry, in casks. Eight percent of the gross weight; in oil in casks, 12 percent of the gross weight.

Pimientos in tins imported from Spain.

Size can	Drained weights
3 kilo.	13.6 kilograms (30 lb.)—case of 6 tins
794 grams (28 oz.)	16.7 kilograms (36.7 lb.)—case of 24 tins
425 grams (15 oz.)	8.0 kilograms (17.72 lb.)—case of 24 tins
198 grams (7 oz.)	3.9 kilograms (8.62 lb.)—case of 24 tins
113 grams (4 oz.)	2.4 kilograms (5.33 lb.)—case of 24 tins

Tobacco, leaf not stemmed, 59 kilograms (13 lb.) per bale; Sumatra: actual tare for outside coverings, plus 1.9 kilograms ($4^{1}/_{4}$ lb.) for the inside matting and, if a certificate is attached to the invoice certifying that the bales contain paper wrappings and specifying whether light or heavy paper has been used, either 113 grams (4 oz.) or 227 grams (8 oz.) for the paper wrapping according to the thickness of paper used.

For other goods dutiable on the net weight an actual tare will be determined. An accurate tare stated on the invoice is acceptable for Customs purposes in certain circumstances.

If the importer of record files a timely application with the district or port director of Customs, an allowance may be made in any case for excessive moisture and impurities not usually found in or upon the particular kind of goods.

5   packing of goods—commingling

Packing

Information on how to pack goods for the purposes of transporting may be obtained from shipping manuals, carriers, forwarding agents, and other sources. This chapter, therefore, deals with packing goods being exported in a way which will permit U.S. Customs officers to examine, weigh, measure, and release the goods promptly.

Orderly packing and proper invoicing go hand in hand. You will speed up the clearance of your goods through customs, if you:

Invoice your goods in a systematic manner.

Show the exact quantity of each item of goods in each box, bale, case or other package.

Put marks and numbers on each package.

Show those marks or numbers on your invoice opposite the itemization of goods contained in the package which bears those marks and numbers.

When the packages contain goods of one kind only, or when the goods are imported in packages the contents and values of which are uniform, the designation of packages for examination and the examination for customs purposes is greatly facilitated. If the contents and values differ from package to package, the possibility of delay and confusion is increased. Sometimes, because of the kinds of goods or because of the unsystematic manner in which they are packed, the entire shipment must be examined.

Pack and invoice your goods in a manner which makes a speedy examination possible. Always bear in mind that it may not be possible to ascertain the contents of your packages without full examination unless your invoice clearly shows the marks and numbers on each package (whether box, case, or bale) and specifies the exact quantity of each item of adequately described goods in each marked and numbered package.

Also, be aware that Customs examines cargo for narcotics that may be hidden in cargo, unbeknownst to the shipper or the importer. This can be time-consuming and expensive for both the importer and the Customs Service. Narcotics inspections require completely stripping a container in order to physically examine a large portion of the cargo. This labor-intensive handling of cargo, whether by Customs, labor organizations, or private individuals, results in added costs, increased delays, and possible damage to the product. Importers can expedite this inspection process by working with Customs to develop packing standards that will permit effective Customs examinations with a minimum of delay, damage, and cost.

A critical aspect in facilitating inspections is the way in which cargo is loaded. "Palletizing" cargo—loading it onto pallets or other consolidated units—is an effective way to expedite such examinations. Palletization allows for quick cargo removal, or "devanning" of containers, in minutes instead of the hours it takes to use a forklift. Another example is leaving enough space at the top of a container and an aisle down the center to allow access by a narcotic-detector dog.

Your cooperation in these respects will help the Customs officers to decide which packages must be opened and examined; how much weighing, counting, or measuring must be done and whether the goods are properly marked. It will simplify the ascertainment of tare and reduce the number of samples to be taken for laboratory analysis or for any other customs purpose. It will facilitate the verification of the contents of the packages as well as the reporting by Customs officers of missing or excess goods. And it will minimize the possibility that the importer may be asked to redeliver for examination packages which were released to him on the theory that the packages designated for examination were sufficient for that purpose.

It is clear that packing which, in fact, amounts to a confusion of different kinds of goods makes it impracticable for Customs officers to determine the quantity of each kind of product in an importation and leads to various complications. No problem arises from the orderly packing of several kinds of properly invoiced goods in one package—it is indiscriminate packing which causes difficulty.

Commingling

Except as mentioned hereafter, whenever articles subject to different rates of duty are so packed together or mingled such that the quantity or value of each class of articles cannot be readily ascertained by Customs officers (without physical segregation of the shipment or the contents of any package thereof) the commingled articles shall be subject to the highest rate of duty applicable to any part of the commingled lot, unless the consignee or his agent segregates under Customs supervision.

The three methods of ready ascertainment specified by General Note 6, HTSUS, are (1) sampling, (2) verification of packing lists or other documents filed at the time of entry, or (3) evidence showing performance of commercial settlements tests generally accepted in the trade and filed in the time and manner as prescribed in the Customs Regulations.

The segregation is at the risk and expense of the consignee. It must be done within 30 days (unless a longer time is granted) after the date of personal delivery or the date of mailing of a notice to the consignee by the district or port director of Customs that the goods are commingled. The compensation and expenses of the Customs officers supervising the segregation must be paid for by the consignee.

Assessment of duty on the commingled lot at the highest applicable rate does not apply to any part of a shipment if the consignee or his agent furnishes satisfactory proof that (1) such part is commercially negligible, is not capable of segregation without excessive cost, and will not be segregated prior to its use in a manufacturing process or otherwise, and (2) the commingling was not intended to avoid the payment of lawful duties.

Any article for which such proof is furnished shall be considered for all Customs purposes as a part of the article, subject to the next lower rate of duty, with which it is commingled.

In addition, the highest rate rule mentioned does not apply to any part of a shipment if there is furnished satisfactory proof that (1) the value of the commingled articles is less than the aggregate value would be if the shipment were segregated, (2) the shipment is not capable of segregation without excessive cost and will not be segregated prior to its use in a manufacturing process or otherwise, and (3) the commingling was not intended to avoid the payment of lawful duties.

Any merchandise for which such proof is furnished shall be considered for all Customs purposes to be dutiable at the rate applicable to the material present in greater quantity than any other material.

The above rules do not apply if the tariff schedules provide a particular tariff treatment for commingled articles.

6 commercial invoice

A commercial invoice, signed by the seller or shipper, or his agent, is acceptable for customs purposes if it is prepared in accordance with Section 141.86, Customs Regulations, and in the manner customary for a commercial transaction involving goods of the kind covered by the invoice.

The invoice must provide the following information, as required by the Tariff Act:

(1) The port of entry to which the merchandise is destined;

(2) If merchandise is sold or agreed to be sold, the time, place, and names of buyer and seller; if consigned, the time and origin of shipment, and names of shipper and receiver;

(3) A detailed description of the merchandise, including the name by which each item is known, the grade or quality, and the marks, numbers, and symbols under which sold by the seller or manufacturer to the trade in the country of exportation, together with the marks and numbers of the packages in which the merchandise is packed;

(4) The quantities in weights and measures;

(5) If sold or agreed to be sold, the purchase price of each item in the currency of the sale;

(6) If the merchandise is shipped for consignment, the value for each item, in the currency in which the transactions are usually made or, in the absence of such value, the price in such currency that the manufacturer, seller, shipper, or owner would have received, or was willing to receive, for such merchandise if sold in the ordinary course of trade and in the usual wholesale quantities in the country of exportation;

(7) The kind of currency;

(8) All charges upon the merchandise, itemized by name and amount including freight, insurance, commission, cases, containers, coverings, and cost of packing; and if not included above, all charges, costs, and expenses incurred in bringing the merchandise from alongside the carrier at the first U.S. port of entry. The cost of packing, cases, containers, and inland freight to the port of exportation need not be itemized by amount if included in the invoice price and so identified. Where the required information does not appear on the invoice as originally prepared, it shall be shown on an attachment to the invoice;

(9) All rebates, drawbacks, and bounties, separately itemized, allowed upon the exportation of the merchandise;

(10) The country of origin; and

(11) All goods or services furnished for the production of the merchandise not included in the invoice price.

If the merchandise on the documents is sold while in transit, the original invoice reflecting this transaction and the resale invoice or a statement of sale showing the price paid for each item by the purchaser shall be filed as part of the entry, entry summary, or withdrawal documentation.

The invoice and all attachments must be in the English language, or shall be accompanied by an accurate English translation.

Each invoice shall state in adequate detail what merchandise is contained in each individual package.

If the invoice or entry does not disclose the weight, gage, or measure of the merchandise necessary to ascertain duties, the consignee shall pay expenses incurred to obtain this information prior to the release of the merchandise from Customs custody.

Each invoice shall set forth in detail, for each class or kind of merchandise, every discount from list or other base price which has been or may be allowed in fixing each purchaser price or value.

When more than one invoice is included in the same entry, each invoice with its attachments shall be numbered consecutively by the importer on the bottom of the face of each page, beginning with number 1. If invoice is more than two pages, begin with number 1 for the first page of the first invoice and continue in a single series of numbers through all the invoices and attachments included in one entry. If an entry covers one invoice of one page and a second invoice of two pages, the numbering at the bottom of the page shall be as follows: Inv. 1, p.1; Inv. 2, p.2; Inv. 2, p.3.

Any information required on an invoice may be set forth either on the invoice or on the attachment.

Specific Requirements

1. Separate Invoice Required for Each Shipment. Not more than one distinct shipment from one consignor to one consignee by one commercial carrier shall be included on the same invoice.

2. Assembled Shipments. Merchandise assembled for shipment to the same consignee by one commercial carrier may be included in one invoice. The original bills or invoices covering the merchandise, or extracts therefrom, showing the actual price paid or agreed to be paid, should be attached to the invoice.

3. Installment Shipments. Installments of a shipment covered by a single order or contract and shipped from one consignor to one consignee may be included in one invoice if the installments arrive at the port of entry by any means of transportation within a period not to exceed 10 consecutive days.

The invoice should be prepared in the same manner as are invoices covering single shipments and should include any additional information which may be required for the particular class of goods concerned. If it is practical to do so, the invoice should show the quantities, values, and other invoice data with respect to each installment, and the identification of the importing conveyance in which each installment was shipped.

4. Production "Assist." The invoice should indicate whether the production of merchandise involved costs for "assists" (i.e.—dies, molds, tooling, printing plates, artwork, engineering work, design and development, financial assistance, etc.) which are not included in the invoice price. If assists were involved, state their value, if known, and by whom supplied. Were they supplied without cost, or on a rental basis, or were they invoiced separately? If the latter, attach a copy of the invoice.

Whenever U.S. Customs requires information on the cost of production of goods for customs valuation, the importer will be notified by the district director. Thereafter, invoices covering shipments of such goods must contain a statement on the cost of production by the manufacturer or producer.

5. Additional Information Required. Special information may be required on certain goods or classes of goods in addition to the information normally required on the invoice. Although the United States importer usually advises the exporter of these special situations, section 141.89 of the Customs Regulations, which covers the requirements for these goods, has been reproduced in the appendix.

6. Rates of Exchange. For merchandise imported from a country having a currency for which two or more rates of exchange have been certified by the Federal Reserve Bank of New York (section 522 of the Tariff Act of 1930), the invoice will show the exchange rate or rates used in converting the United States dollars received for the merchandise into the foreign currency and the percentage of each rate if two or more rates are used. If a rate or combination of rates used in payment of costs, charges, or expenses is different from those used in payment for the merchandise, state that rate or combination of rates separately. Where dollars have not been converted at the time the invoice is prepared, that fact is stated on the invoice, in which case the invoice shall also state the rate or combination of rates at which the dollars will be converted or that it is not known what rate or rates will be used. Rates of exchange are not required for merchandise unconditionally free of duty or subject only to a specific rate of duty not depending on value.

7 other invoices

Pro Forma Invoice

If the required commercial invoice is not filed at the time the merchandise is entered, a statement in the form of an invoice (a pro forma invoice) must be filed by the importer at the time of entry. A bond is given for production of the required invoice not later than 120 days from the date of entry. If the invoice is needed for statistical purposes, it must generally be produced within 50 days from the date the entry summary is required to be filed.

The exporter should bear in mind that unless he forwards the required invoice in time, the American importer will incur a liability under his bond for failure to file the invoice with the district or port director of Customs before the expiration of the 120-day period.

Although a pro forma invoice is not a document which is prepared by the exporter, it is of interest to exporters as it gives a general idea as to the kind of information needed for entry purposes and indicates what the importer may find necessary to furnish Customs officers at the time a formal entry is filed for a commercial shipment if a properly prepared customs or commercial invoice is not available at the time the goods are entered. An acceptable format for a pro forma invoice is reproduced in the appendix.

Some of the additional information specified for commodities under section 141.89 of the Customs Regulations may not be required when entry is made on a pro forma invoice. However, the pro forma invoice must contain sufficient data for examination, classification, and appraisement purposes.

Special Invoices   Special invoices are required for some merchandise, for example, some articles of steel. See 141.89 CR.

8   frequent errors in invoicing

If difficulties, delays, and possible penal sanctions affecting the importer are to be avoided, due care must be exercised by foreign sellers and shippers in the preparation of invoices and other documents to be used in the entry of goods into the commerce of the United States. Each document must contain all information required by law or regulations, and every statement of fact contained in the documents must be true and accurate. Any inaccurate or misleading statement of fact in a document presented to a Customs officer in connection with an entry, or the omission from the document of required information, may result in delays in merchandise release, the detention of the goods or a claim against the importer for forfeiture value. Even though the inaccuracy or omission was unintentional, the importer may be required to establish that he exercised due diligence and was not negligent, in order to avoid sanctions with consequent delay in obtaining possession of goods and closing the transaction.

It is particularly important that all statements relating to merchandise description, price or value and amounts of discounts, charges, and commissions be truthfully and accurately set forth. It is also important that the invoices shall set forth the true name of the actual seller and purchaser of the goods, in the case of purchased goods, or the true name of the actual consignor and consignee, when the goods are shipped otherwise than in pursuance of a purchase. It is important, too, that the invoice shall otherwise reflect the real nature of the transaction pursuant to which the goods were shipped to the United States.

The fundamental rule is that the shipper and importer must furnish the Customs officers with all pertinent information with respect to each import transaction to assist the Custom officers in determining the tariff status of the goods. Examples of omissions and inaccuracies to be avoided are:

The shipper assumes that a commission, royalty, or other charge against the goods is a so-called "nondutiable" item and omits it from the invoice.

A foreign shipper who purchases goods and sells them to a United States importer at a delivered price shows on the invoice the cost of the goods to him instead of the delivered price.

A foreign shipper manufactures goods partly with the use of materials supplied by the United States importer, but invoices the goods at the actual cost to the manufacturer without including the value of the materials supplied by the importer.

The foreign manufacturer ships replacement goods to his customer in the United States and invoices the goods at the net price without showing the full price less the allowance for defective goods previously shipped and returned.

A foreign shipper who sells goods at list price, less a discount, invoices them at the net price, and fails to show the discount.

A foreign shipper sells goods at a delivered price but invoices them at a price f.o.b. the place of shipment and omits the subsequent charges.

A foreign shipper indicates in the invoice that the importer is the purchaser, whereas he is in fact either an agent who is receiving a commission for selling the goods or a party who will receive part of the proceeds of the sale of the goods sold for the joint account of the shipper and consignee.

Invoice descriptions are vague, listing only part numbers, truncated or coded descriptions, or lumping various articles together as one when several distinct items are included.

9 dutiable status of goods

Rates of Duty

All goods imported into the United States are subject to duty or duty-free entry in accordance with their classification under the applicable items in the Harmonized Tariff Schedule of the United States. An annotated, looseleaf edition of the tariff schedule may be purchased from the U.S. Government Printing Office, Washington, D.C. 20402. The tariff schedule may also be found in 19 U.S.C.A. sec. 1202.

When goods are dutiable, ad valorem, specific, or compound rates may be assessed. An ad valorem rate, which is the type of rate most often applied, is a percentage of value of the merchandise, such as 5 percent ad valorem. A specific rate is a specified amount per unit of weight or other quantity, such as 5.9 cents per dozen. A compound rate is a combination of both an ad valorem rate and a specific rate, such as 0.7 cents per pound plus 10 percent ad valorem.

Free of Duty or Dutiable

Rates of duty for imported merchandise may also vary depending upon the country of origin. Most merchandise is dutiable under the most-favored-nation (MFN) rates in the General column under column 1 of the tariff schedule. Merchandise from countries to which the MFN rates have not been extended is dutiable at the full or "statutory" rates in column 2 of the tariff schedules.

Free rates are provided for many subheadings in columns 1 and 2 of the tariff schedule. Duty-free status is also available under various conditional exemptions which are reflected in the Special column under column 1 of the tariff schedule. One of the more frequently applied exemptions from duty occurs under the Generalized System of Preferences. GSP-eligible merchandise qualifies for duty-free entry when it is from a beneficiary developing country and meets other requirements as discussed in Chapter 13. Other exemptions are found under subheadings in Chapter 98 of the tariff schedule. These subheadings include, among other provisions, certain personal exemptions, exemptions for articles for scientific or other institutional purposes, and exemptions for returned American goods.

Rulings on Imports

The Customs Service makes its decision as to the dutiable status of merchandise when the entry is liquidated after the entry documents have been filed. When advance information is needed, do not depend on a small "trial" or "test" shipment since there is no guarantee that the next shipment will receive the same tariff treatment. Small importations may slip by, particularly if they are processed under informal procedures which apply to small shipments or in circumstances warranting application of a flat rate. An exporter, importer, or other interested party may get advance information on any matter affecting the dutiable status of merchandise by writing the district director where the merchandise will be entered or to the Regional Commissioner of Customs, New York Region, New York, N.Y. 10048 or to the U.S. Customs Service. Attention: Office of Regulations and Rulings, Washington, D.C. 20229. Detailed information on the procedures applicable to decisions on prospective importations is given in 19 CFR part 177.

Binding Decisions

While you will find that, for many purposes, the ports and districts are your best sources of information, informal information obtained on tariff classifications is not binding. The importing public may obtain a binding tariff classification ruling, which can be relied upon for placing or accepting orders or for making other business determinations, under Chapters 1 through 97 of the Harmonized Tariff Schedule (HTS) by writing to any Customs district director or to the Area Director of Customs, New York Seaport, 6 World Trade Center, New York, N.Y. 10048. The rulings will be binding at all ports of entry unless revoked by the Customs Service's Office of Regulations and Rulings.

The following information is required in ruling requests:

1. The names, addresses and other identifying information of all interested parties (if known) and the manufacturer ID code (if known).

2. The name(s) of the port(s) in which the merchandise will be entered (if known).

3. A description of the transaction, for example, a prospective importation of (merchandise) from (country).

4. A statement that there are, to the importer's knowledge, no issues on the commodity pending before the Customs Service or any court.

5. A statement as to whether classification advice had previously been sought from a Customs officer, and if so, from whom, and what advice was rendered, if any.

A request for a tariff classification should include the following information:

1. A complete description of the goods. Send samples, if practical, sketches, diagrams, or other illustrative material that will be useful in supplementing the written description.

2. Cost breakdowns of component materials and their respective quantities shown in percentages, if possible.

3. A description of the principal use of the goods, as a class or kind of merchandise, in the United States.

4. Information as to commercial, scientific or common designations as may be applicable.

5. Any other information that may be pertinent or required for the purpose of tariff classification.

Any of the first four requirements above may be disregarded if you are certain the information will not be of use for tariff classification purposes. However, to avoid delays, your request should be as complete as possible. If you send a sample, do not rely on that to tell the whole story. Also, please note that samples may be subjected to laboratory analysis, which is done free of charge. However, if a sample is destroyed during laboratory analysis, then, of course, it cannot be returned.

Information submitted and incorporated in the response to a request for a Customs decision may be disclosed or withheld in accordance with the provisions of the Freedom of Information Act, as amended (15 U.S.C. 552; 19 CFR 177.8(a)(3)).

Protests

The importer may disagree with the dutiable status after the entry has been liquidated. A decision at this stage of the entry transaction is requested by filing a protest and application for further review on Customs Form 19 within 90 days after liquidation (see 19 CFR part 174). If the Customs Service denies a protest, dutiable status may then be determined through litigation against the Government.

Liability for Duties

There is no provision under which U.S. duties or taxes may be prepaid in a foreign country before exportation to the United States. This is true even in the case of gifts sent through the mail.

In the usual case, liability for the payment of duty becomes fixed at the time an entry for consumption or for warehouse is filed with Customs. The obligation for payment is upon the person or firm in whose name the entry is filed. When goods have been entered for warehouse, the liability for the payment of duties may be transferred to any person who purchases the goods and desires to withdraw them in his own name.

Payment to a Customs broker will not relieve an importer of record of liability for Customs charges (duties, taxes, and other debts owing Customs) in the event the charges are not paid by the broker. Therefore, if the importer pays by check, Customs charges may be paid with a separate check payable to "U.S. Customs Service" which will be delivered to Customs by the broker.

If the entry is made in the name of a Customs broker, relief from statutory liability for the payment of increased or additional duties found due may be obtained by the broker if (1) the actual owner of goods is named and (2) the owner's declaration whereby the owner agrees to pay the additional amount of duty and the owner's bond are filed by the broker with the district director within 90 days of the date of entry.

10   containers or holders

Lift vans, cargo vans, shipping tanks, pallets and certain articles used in the shipment of goods in international traffic are designated as "instruments of international traffic" by the Customs Service. So long as this designation applies, they are not subject to entry or duty when they arrive, whether they are loaded or empty. Holders of merchandise, but of a different class, may also be designated as instruments of international traffic upon application to the Commissioner of Customs. However, any article designated as an instrument of international traffic must be entered and duty paid, if applicable, if it is diverted to a domestic use.

Containers specially shaped or fitted to contain a specific article or set of articles, suitable for long-term use and entered with the articles for which they are intended, are classifiable with the accompanying articles if they are of a kind normally sold therewith. Examples of such containers are: camera cases, musical instrument cases, gun cases, drawing instrument cases, and necklace cases. This rule does not apply to containers which give the importation as a whole its essential character.

Subject to the above rule, packing materials and packing containers entered with goods packed in them are classified with these goods if they are of a kind normally used for packing such goods. However, this does not apply to packing materials or containers that are clearly suitable for repetitive use.

11   temporary free importations

Temporary Importation Under Bond (TIB)

Goods of the types enumerated below when not imported for sale or for sale on approval may be admitted into the United States without the payment of duty, under bond, for their exportation within one year from the date of importation. Generally, the amount of the bond is double the estimated duties. The one-year period for exportation may, upon application to the district or port director, be extended for one or more further periods which, when added to the initial one year, shall not exceed a total of three years. There is an exception in the case of articles covered in item 15: the period of the bond may not exceed six months and may not be extended.

Merchandise entered under TIB must be exported before expiration of the bond period, or any extension, to avoid assessment of liquidated damages in the amount of the bond.

Classes of Goods

1. Merchandise to be repaired, altered, or processed (including processes which result in a article being manufactured or produced in the United States), provided that the following conditions are met:

   a. The merchandise will not be processed into an article manufactured or produced in the United States if the article is (1) potable grain alcohol, distilled spirits, wine, beer, or any dilution or mixture of these; (2) a perfume or other commodity containing ethyl alcohol whether denatured or not; (3) a product of wheat.

   b. If merchandise is processed and results in an article being manufactured or produced in the United States other than those described above, (1) a complete accounting will be made to the Customs Service for all articles, wastes, and irrecoverable losses resulting from the processing, and (2) all articles will be exported or destroyed under Customs supervision within the bonded period. Valuable waste must also be exported or so destroyed unless duty, if applicable, is paid.

2. Models of wearing apparel imported by manufacturers for use solely as models in their own establishments may require quota compliance.

3. Articles imported by illustrators and photographers for use solely as models in their own establishments to illustrate catalogs, pamphlets, or advertising matter.

4. Samples solely for use in taking orders for merchandise may require quota compliance.

5. Articles solely for examination with a view to reproduction or for examination and reproduction (except photoengraved printing plates for examination and reproduction); and motion-picture advertising films.

6. Articles intended solely for testing, experimental, or review purposes, including plans, specifications, drawings, blueprints, photographs, and articles for use in connection with experiments or for study. If articles under this category are destroyed in connection with the experiment or study, proof must be presented to satisfy the obligation under the bond to export the articles.

7. Automobiles, motorcycles, bicycles, airplanes, airships, balloons, boats, racing shells, and similar vehicles and craft, and the usual equipment of the foregoing, if brought temporarily into the United States by nonresidents for the purpose of taking part in races or other specific contests. District or port directors may defer the exaction of a bond for a period not to exceed 90 days after the date of importation for vehicles and craft to take part in races or other specific contests for other than money purposes. If the vehicle or craft is not exported or the bond is not given within the period of such deferment, the vehicle or craft shall be subject to forfeiture.

8. Locomotives and other railroad equipment brought temporarily into the United States for use in clearing obstructions, fighting fires, or making emergency repairs on railroads within the United States, for use in transportation otherwise than in international traffic when the Secretary of the Treasury finds that the temporary use of foreign railroad equipment is necessary to meet an emergency.

9. Containers for compressed gases, filled or empty, and containers or other articles in use for covering or holding merchandise (including personal or household effects) during transportation and suitable for reuse for that purpose.

10. Professional equipment, tools of trade, repair components for equipment or tools admitted under this item, and camping equipment imported by or for nonresidents sojourning temporarily in the United States for the nonresident's use, or by an organization represented by the nonresident which is a legally established business in a foreign country.

11. Articles of special design for temporary use exclusively in connection with the manufacture or production of articles for export.

12. Animals and poultry brought into the United States for the purpose of breeding, exhibition, or competition for prizes, and the usual equipment therefor.

13. Theatrical scenery, properties, and apparel brought into the United States by proprietors or managers of theatrical exhibitions arriving from abroad for temporary use by them in such exhibitions.

14. Works of free fine arts, drawings, engravings, photographic pictures, and philosophical and scientific apparatus brought into the United States by professional artists, lecturers, or scientists arriving from abroad for use by them for exhibition and in illustration, promotion, and encouragement of art, science or industry in the United States.

15. Automobiles, automobile chassis, automobile bodies, cutaway portions of any of the foregoing, and parts for any of the foregoing, finished, unfinished, or cutaway, when intended solely for show purposes. These articles may be admitted only on condition that the Secretary of the Treasury has found that the foreign country from which the articles were imported allows or will allow substantially reciprocal privileges in respect of similar imports to that country from the United States. If the Secretary finds that a foreign country has discontinued or will discontinue the allowance of such privileges, the privileges under this item shall not apply thereafter to imports from that country.

Relief from Liability

Relief from liability under bond may be obtained in any case in which the articles are destroyed under Customs supervision, in lieu of exportation, within the original bond period. However, in the case of articles entered under item 6, destruction need not be under Customs supervision where articles are destroyed during the course of experiments or tests during the bond period or any lawful extension, but satisfactory proof of destruction shall be furnished to the district or port director with whom the customs entry is filed.

ATA Carnet

ATA stands for the combined French and English words "Admission Temporaire—Temporary Admission." ATA carnet is an international customs document which may be used for the temporary duty-free importation of certain goods into a country in lieu of the usual customs documents required. The carnet serves as a guarantee against the payment of customs duties which may become due on goods temporarily imported and not re-exported. Quota compliance may be required on certain types of merchandise. ATA textile carnets are subject to quota and visa requirements.

A carnet is valid for one year. The traveler or businessman, however, may make as many trips as desired during the period the carnet is valid provided he has sufficient pages for each stop.

The United States currently allows ATA carnets to be used for the temporary admission of professional equipment, commercial samples, and advertising material. Most other countries allow the use of carnets for the temporary admission of these goods and, in some cases, other uses of the ATA carnet are permitted. ATA carnets can also be used for transit (in-bond movement of goods) in the United States under the applicable regulations, 19 CFR part 114.

Local carnet associations, as members of the International Bureau of the Paris-based International Chamber of Commerce, issue carnets to their residents. These associations guarantee the payment of duties to local customs authorities should goods imported under cover of a foreign-issued carnet not be re-exported. In the United States, the U.S. Council of the International Chamber of Commerce, located at 1212 Avenue of the Americas, New York, N.Y. 10036, (212) 354–4480, has been designated by U.S. Customs as the United States issuing and guaranteeing organization. A fee is charged by the Council for its service.

ATA carnets can be used in the following countries:

Algeria	Hungary	Norway
Australia	Iceland	Poland
Austria	India	Portugal
Belgium	Iran	Romania
Bulgaria	Ireland	Senegal
Canada	Israel	Singapore
Canary Islands	Italy	South Africa
Cyprus	Ivory Coast	Spain
Czechoslovakia	Japan	Sri Lanka
Denmark	Republic of South Korea	Sweden
Finland	Luxembourg	Switzerland
France	Malaysia	Turkey
Germany	Malta	United Kingdom
Gibraltar	Mauritius	United States
Greece	Netherlands	Yugoslavia
Hong Kong	New Zealand	

Egypt and certain other countries have accepted the ATA convention but have not implemented the use of carnets.

As countries are being continuously added to the carnet system, please check with the U.S. Council if a country you wish to visit is not included in the above list.

12   u.s./canada free trade agreement (fta)

The provisions of the U.S./Canada Free Trade Agreement were adopted by the United States with the enactment of the United States-Canada Free Trade Agreement Implementation Act of 1988 (100 Stat. 418, Public Law 100-449). Nineteen CFR Parts 10, 24, and 148 of the Customs Regulations contain amendments to implement the duty preferences on the FTA. The FTA not only reduced tariffs on imported merchandise between Canada and the United States, but it opened up new areas of trade in investment services, agriculture, and business travel.

The agreement is divided into 8 parts setting out provisions (Articles) relating to its objectives. The most obvious aspect of the FTA is the mechanism set up to progressively eliminate remaining tariffs over a ten-year period for goods that originate in the U.S. or Canada. These reductions were divided into four categories: Category A, immediate elimination on January 1, 1989; Category B, elimination in five cuts of 20% each year beginning January 1, 1989; Category C, eliminated in ten cuts of 10% each year beginning January 1, 1989; and Category D, which were already existing free duty rates. Also included in the Articles is the provision for accelerated reduction upon petition by industries in either country. These provisions have been utilized both in 1990 and 1991.

In an effort to eliminate tariffs on eligible goods traded between the U.S. and Canada, and to preclude third countries from obtaining tariff benefits by merely passing goods through the U.S. or Canada, Rules of Origin were devised. These rules are for determining origin for FTA eligibility and not for country of origin determination in other areas such as marking, quota, dumping and countervailing duty assessment.

Article 301, Chapter 5 of the FTA, spells out four general rules of origin that apply to all goods. It should be understood that the FTA defines originating as "qualifying under the rules of origin set out in Chapter 3". To "originate" means that goods obtain FTA tariff treatment in accordance with the rules of origin. Use of the word "origin" within the context of the FTA is different from determining country of origin. It is possible, for instance, for merchandise not to "originate" in Canada as set forth in the FTA, but still be Canadian articles for the purpose of determining the proper country of origin for other trade programs.

The General Rules of Origin for FTA eligibility are:

a. Goods wholly of U.S. or Canadian origin.

b. Goods meet the requirements of the specific rules:

    (1) through a classification change alone (this may be accomplished by processing or assembly, e.g. crude rubber from Malaysia processed into tires) or,

    (2) through a classification change and the application of a value test. (This can mean that the value of the materials originating in the territory, plus the direct cost of processing performed in the territory, constitute a certain minimum percentage of the product—50% for most products, 70% for pesticides. The costs of processing used are those costs *directly* related to the production of the article. This does not include any general expenses.

c. Goods assembled from parts which take the same classification as the finished article, and they meet a value test, except for textile articles in Chapters 61–63 of the HTS.

d. Normal accessories, spare parts, or tools delivered with FTA-eligible equipment, machinery apparatus, or vehicles form part of its standard equipment and the quantities and values of such accessories, spare parts, or tools are customary for the equipment, machinery, apparatus, or vehicle.

e. A commodity-specific rule in the Harmonized Tariff Schedule takes precedence over a General Rule.

In order to be eligible for FTA treatment, goods must not enter the commerce of a third country. If FTA–eligible goods are shipped through a third country, they must remain under Customs' control. They may only undergo handling related to unloading, reloading, and any operation to preserve them in good condition. The shipping documentation must show the U.S. or Canada as the final destination. Any type of processing in a third country, no matter how minimal, will remove the FTA eligibility from the article.

Entry Procedures

As with other trade preference programs, the importer must make claim for FTA in order to receive the tariff treatment. An importer makes a claim by:

1. Prefixing "CA" to the tariff classification number.

2. Signing the CF 7501, Entry Summary.

Exporters Certificate of Origin

FTA Chapter 4, Annex 406, Customs Administration, requires that an importer base his claim on the exporter's written certificate of origin. This may be CF 353, **EXPORTERS CERTIFICATE OF ORIGIN**, or the Canadian version (Canadian Form B-151). This certificate may be presented on an entry-by-entry basis or may be utilized as a blanket declaration for a period of 12 months.

Special Provisions for Sensitive Sectors

Under FTA rules, most textile products must undergo a two-step process in order to be considered goods originating in the territory. For example yarn imported into the territory from a third country would have to be woven or knitted into a fabric and then cut and sewn into a garment or article before the garment or article would be considered originating goods.

A tariff rate quota is available to grant FTA treatment to specified quantities of apparel goods and fabric that undergo only a one-step process.

Additional detailed information is contained in the book "U.S./CANADA FREE TRADE AGREEMENT," Publication No. 592, February 1991.

13 generalized system of preferences (gsp)

The Generalized System of Preferences is a program providing for free rates of duty for merchandise from beneficiary developing independent countries and dependent countries and territories to encourage their economic growth (see below). This program was enacted by the United States in the Trade Act of 1974, became effective on January 1, 1976, and was extended to July 4, 1993.

Eligible Items

The GSP eligibility list contains a wide range of products classifiable under approximately 3,000 different subheadings in the Harmonized Tariff Schedule of the United States. These items are identified either by an "A" or "A*" in the "Special" column under column 1 of the tariff schedule. Merchandise classifiable under a subheading designated in this manner may qualify for duty-free entry if imported into the United States directly from any of the designated countries and territories. Merchandise from one or more of these countries, however, may be excluded from the exemption if there is an "A*" in the "Special" column. The list of countries and exclusions, as well as the list of GSP-eligible articles, will change from time to time over the life of the program. Therefore, the latest edition of the Harmonized Tariff Schedules of the United States will contain the most up-to-date information.

If advance tariff classification information is needed to ascertain whether or not your commodity is eligible under the GSP, you may obtain this information under the procedures previously discussed in Chapter 9 relating to dutiable status.

Formal Entries

For commercial shipments requiring a formal entry, a claim for duty-free status is made under GSP by showing on the entry summary that the country of origin is a designated beneficiary developing country and by showing an "A" with the appropriate GSP-eligible subheading. Eligible merchandise will be entitled to duty-free treatment provided the following conditions are met:

1. The merchandise must be destined to the United States without contingency for diversion at the time of exportation from the beneficiary developing country.

2. The UNCTAD (United Nations Conference on Trade and Development) Certificate of Origin Form A must be properly prepared, signed by the exporter and either be filed with the entry or furnished before liquidation or other final action on the entry if requested to do so by Customs.

3. The merchandise must be imported directly into the United States from the beneficiary country. In addition, the cost or value of materials produced in the beneficiary developing country and/or the direct cost of processing performed there must represent at least 35 percent of the appraised value of the goods.

The cost or value of materials imported into the beneficiary development country may be included in calculating the 35 percent value-added requirement for an eligible article if the materials are first substantially transformed into new and different articles and are then used as constituent materials in the production of the eligible article. The phrase "direct costs of processing" includes costs directly incurred or reasonably allocated to the processing of the article, such as the cost of all actual labor, dies, molds, tooling, depreciation on machinery, research and development and inspection and testing. Business overhead, administrative expenses, salaries, and profit, as well as general business expenses, such as administrative salaries, casualty and liability insurance, advertising and salesmen's salaries, are not considered as direct costs of processing.

Certificate of Origin Form A

Normally, the Customs Service will accept an entry at the free rate, whether or not the Form A is presented at the time of entry. If Form A is not available, the importer **will have to produce it for GSP duty-free treatment if requested to do so by Customs.**

The UNCTAD Certificate of Origin Form A is not available for sale in the United States. The beneficiary developing countries and territories participating in the program are responsible for printing and supplying this form. Exporters may get this form from the appropriate government authority in their respective countries. If Form A is not available from the governmental certifying authority, the form may be purchased from any of the commercial printers listed below, or you may contact the Director, Technical Assistant Project/GSP, UNCTAD, 1211 Geneva 10, Switzerland, for further advice on obtaining the form.

Germany
—Formular-Verlag Purschke & Hensel
  Barbacher Strass 232
  D-5300 Bonn

—Wilhelm Kohler Verlag
  495 Minden 2
  Postfach 1530
  Bruckenkopf 2a

Hong Kong
—Che San & Company
  10 Pottinger Street

—Cheung Lee Printing Company
  210 A Li Po Chun Chambers
  185-195 Des Voeux Road, Central

—Winson (HK) Printing Company
  80-82 Wharf Road
  North Point

Informal Entries

Although Certificates of Origin Form A are not required for merchandise covered by an informal entry, the district director of Customs may require such other evidence of the country of origin as he may deem necessary. The requirement of Form A for merchandise covered by a formal entry may be waived by the district director where he determines appropriate, or if the imported articles are for household or personal use and are not intended for resale or brought in for the account of others, or if the district director is otherwise satisfied that the merchandise qualifies for duty-free treatment under GSP.

Sources of Additional Information

Customs rules and regulations on GSP are incorporated in sections 10.171-10.178 of the Customs Regulations. Address any question you may have as to the administrative or operational aspects of the GSP to the Director, Office of Trade Operations, U.S. Customs Service, Washington, D.C. 20229. Requests for information concerning additions to, or deletions from, the list of eligible merchandise under GSP, or the list of beneficiary development countries, should be directed to the Chairman, Trade Policy Staff Subcommittee, Office of U.S. Trade Representative, 600 17th St., N.W., Washington, D.C. 20506.

Generalized System of Preferences (GSP)

Independent Countries

Angola	Ecuador*	Mali	Solomon Islands
Antigua and Barbuda***	Egypt	Malta	Somalia
Argentina	El Salvador	Mauritania	Sri Lanka
Bahamas***	Equatorial Guinea	Mauritius	Sudan
Bahrain	Fiji	Mexico	Surinam
Bangladesh	Gambia	Morocco	Swaziland
Barbados***	Ghana	Mozambique	Syria
Belize***	Grenada***	Namibia	Tanzania
Benin	Guatemala	Nepal	Thailand**
Bhutan	Guinea	Niger	Togo
Bolivia*	Guinea-Bissau	Oman	Tonga
Botswana	Guyana***	Pakistan	Trinidad and Tobago***
Brazil	Haiti	Panama	Tunisia
Burkina Faso	Honduras	Papua, New Guinea	Turkey
Burundi	Hungary	Paraguay	Tuvalu
Cameroon	India	Peru*	Uganda
Cape Verde	Indonesia**	Philippines**	Upper Volta
Central African Republic	Israel	Poland	Uruguay
Chad	Jamaica***	Rwanda	Vanuatu
Colombia*	Jordan	Saint Kitts and	Venezuela*
Comoros	Kenya	Nevis***	Western Samoa
Congo	Kiribati	Saint Lucia***	Yemen Arab Republic
Costa Rica	Lebanon	Saint Vincent and	(Sanaa)
Côte d'Ivoire	Lesotho	the Grenadines***	Yugoslavia
Cyprus	Madagascar	Sao Tome and Principe	Zaire
Djibouti	Malawi	Senegal	Zambia
Dominica***	Malaysia**	Seychelles	Zimbabwe
Dominican Republic	Maldives	Sierra Leone	

Non-Independent Countries and Terrritories

Anguilla	French Polynesia	Pitcairn Islands
Aruba	Gibraltar	Saint Helena
British Indian Ocean Territory	Greenland	Tokelau
Cayman Islands	Heard Island and McDonald Islands	Trust Territory of the Pacific Islands (Palau)
Christmas Island (Australia)	Macau	Turks and Caicos Islands
Cocos (Keeling) Islands	Montserrat***	Virgin Islands, British
Cook Islands	Netherlands Antilles	Wallis and Futuna
Falkland Islands (Islas Malvinas)	New Caledonia	Western Sahara
	Niue	
	Norfolk Island	

* Member countries of the Cartagena Agreement—Andean Group (treated as one country).

** Association of South East Asian Nations—ASEAN (GSP-eligible countries only) treated as one country.

*** Members countries of the Caribbean Common Market—CARICOM (treated as one country).

The Caribbean Basin Initiative (CBI) is a program providing for the duty-free entry of merchandise from designated beneficiary countries or territories. This program was enacted by the United States as the Caribbean Basin Economic Recovery Act, became effective on January 1, 1984, and was permanently extended on October 1, 1990 by the Customs and Trade Act of 1990.

Beneficiary Countries

The following countries and territories have been designated as beneficiary countries for purposes of the CBI:

Antigua and Barbuda
Aruba
Bahamas
Barbados
Belize
Costa Rica
Dominica
Dominican Republic
El Salvador
Grenada
Guatemala
Guyana
Haiti

Honduras
Jamaica
Montserrat
Netherlands Antilles
Nicaragua
Panama
Saint Kitts and Nevis
Saint Lucia
Saint Vincent and the
   Grenadines
Trinidad and Tobago
Virgin Islands, British

Eligible Items

The list of beneficiaries may change from time to time over the life of the program. Therefore, it is necessary to consult General Note (3)(c)(v)(A) in the latest edition of the Harmonized Tariff Schedule of the United States which will contain updated information.

Most products from designated beneficiaries may be eligible for CBI duty-free treatment. These items are identified by either an "E" or "E*" in the Special column under column 1 of the Harmonized Tariff Schedule. Merchandise classifiable under a subheading designated in this manner may qualify for duty-free entry if imported into the United States directly from any of the designated countries and territories. Merchandise from one or more of these countries, however, may be excluded from the exemption if there is an "E*" in the "Special" column. The list of countries may change from time to time over the life of the program. Therefore, the latest edition of the Harmonized Tariff Schedule of the United States will contain the most up-to-date information.

Rules of Origin

Merchandise will be eligible for CBI duty-free treatment only if the following conditions are met:

1. The merchandise must be imported directly from any beneficiary country into the customs territory of the United States.

2. The merchandise must have been produced in a beneficiary country. This requirement is satisfied when (1) the goods are wholly the growth, product, or manufacture of a beneficiary country, or (2) the goods have been substantially transformed into a new and different article of commerce in a beneficiary country.

3. At least 35 percent of the appraised value of the article imported into the United States must consist of the cost or value of materials produced in one or more beneficiary countries and/or the direct costs of processing operations performed in one or more beneficiary countries. The Commonwealth of Puerto Rico and the U.S. Virgin Islands are defined as beneficiary countries for purposes of this requirement; therefore, value attributable to Puerto Rico or the Virgin Islands may also be counted. In addition, the cost or value of materials produced in the customs territory of the United States (other than Puerto Rico) may be counted toward the 35 percent value-added requirement, but only to a maximum of 15 percent of the appraised value of the imported article.

The cost or value of materials imported into a beneficiary country from a non-beneficiary country may be included in calculating the 35 percent value-added requirement for an eligible article if the materials are first substantially transformed into new and different articles of commerce and are then used as constituent materials in the production of the eligible article. The phrase "direct costs of processing operations" includes costs directly incurred or reasonably allocated to the production of the article, such as the cost of actual labor, dies, molds, tooling, depreciation of machinery, research and development, inspection, and testing. Business overhead, administrative expenses, and profit, as well as general business expenses such as casualty and liability insurance, advertising, and salesmen's salaries, are not considered as direct costs of processing operations.

In addition to the origin rules enumerated above, the Customs and Trade Act of 1990 added new criteria for duty-free eligibility under the Caribbean Basin Initiative. First, articles which are the growth, product or manufacture of Puerto Rico and which subsequently are processed in a CBI beneficiary country, may also receive duty-free treatment when entered, if the three following conditions are met:

1. They are imported directly from a beneficiary country into the customs territory of the United States.

2. They are advanced in value or improved in condition by any means in a beneficiary country.

3. Any materials added to the article in a beneficiary country must be a product of a beneficiary country or the U.S.

Second, articles which are assembled or processed in whole from U.S. components or ingredients (other than water) in a beneficiary may be entered free of duty. Duty-free treatment will apply if the components or ingredients are exported directly to the beneficiary country and the finished article is imported directly into the customs territory of the United States.

If advance tariff classification information is needed to ascertain whether or not your merchandise would be eligible for CBI duty-free treatment, you may obtain this information under the procedures previously discussed in Chapter 9 relating to dutiable status.

Formal Entries—Evidence of Country of Origin

For commercial shipments requiring a formal entry, a claim for CBI duty-free treatment is made by showing on the entry summary that the country of origin is a designated beneficiary country and by inserting thereon the letter "E" as prefix to the applicable tariff schedule subheading. In addition, a properly completed Certificate of Origin Form A, as previously discussed in Chapter 13 relating to the Generalized System of Preferences, may be presented at the time of entry; however, the words "Generalized System of Preferences" appearing on the front of the Form A must be replaced by the words "Caribbean Basin Initiative" for purposes of a CBI entry.

Normally, the Customs Service will accept a CBI entry at the free rate whether or not the Form A is presented at the time of entry. If the Form A is not available, the importer will have to produce it for CBI duty-free treatment, if requested to do so by Customs. In addition, where necessary value is added to an article in the United States or Puerto Rico after final exportation of the article from a beneficiary country, a detailed declaration, prepared by the party responsible for the addition of such value, shall be filed in lieu of the Form A as evidence of country of origin. All submitted evidence of country of origin may be subject to such verification as the district director deems necessary.

Informal Entries

Although Certificates of Origin Form A are not required for merchandise covered by an informal entry, the district director may require such other evidence of the country of origin as may be deemed necessary.

Sources of Additional Information

Customs rules and regulations on the CBI are incorporated in sections 10.191-10.198 of the Customs Regulations. Address any question you may have as to the administrative or operational aspects of the CBI to the director of the port or district where the merchandise will be entered or to the Director, Office of Trade Operations, U.S. Customs Service, Washington, D.C. 20229.

15 u.s.-israel free trade area agreement

The United States-Israel Free Trade Area (FTA) agreement is a program providing for free or reduced rates of duty for merchandise from Israel to stimulate trade between the two countries. This program was authorized by the United States in the Trade and Tariff Act of 1984 and implemented by the United States-Israel Free Trade Area Implementation Act of 1985 and Presidential Proclamation 5365 of August 30,1985. The FTA program became effective September 1, 1985, and has no termination date. On January 1, 1995, all currently eligible reduced rate importations from Israel will be accorded duty-free treatment.

Eligible Items

The FTA relates to most tariff items listed in the Harmonized Tariff Schedule of the United States (HTSUS). These items are identified by "I" in the "Special" column under column 1 of the Harmonized Tariff Schedule.

If a claim for duty-free or reduced-duty rates is being made for commercial shipments of Israeli goods covered by a formal entry, the HTSUS subheading must be prefixed with an "I" on the Customs Form 7501 (entry document) or Customs Form 7505 (warehouse withdrawal document), as appropriate.

An article imported into the Customs territory of the United States is eligible for treatment as "Product of Israel" only if:

- That article is the growth, product or manufacture of Israel;

- That article is imported directly from Israel into the Customs territory of the United States;

- The sum of: (1) The cost or value of the materials produced in Israel, plus (2) the direct costs of processing operations performed in Israel is not less than 35 percent of the appraised value of such article at the time it is entered. If the cost or value of materials produced in the customs territory of the United States is included with respect to an eligible article, an amount not to exceed 15 percent of the appraised value of the article at the time it is entered that is attributable to such United States cost or value may be applied toward determining the 35 percent.

- The cost or value of materials imported into Israel from a third country may be included in calculating the 35 percent value-added requirement, provided they are first substantially transformed into new and different articles of commerce and are then used as constituent materials in the production of the eligible article.

No article may be considered to meet these requirements by virtue of having merely undergone:

- Simple combining or packaging operations; or

- Mere dilution with water or mere dilution with another substance that does not materially alter the characteristics of the article.

The phrase "direct costs of processing operations" includes, but is not limited to:

- All actual labor costs involved in the growth, production, manufacture or assembly of the specific merchandise, including fringe benefits, on-the-job training and the costs of engineering, supervisory, quality control and similar personnel.

- Dies, molds, tooling and depreciation on machinery and equipment which are allocable to the specific merchandise.

Direct costs of processing operations do not include costs which are not directly attributable to the merchandise concerned, or are not costs of manufacturing the product, such as (1) profit and (2) general expenses of doing business which are either not allocable to the specific merchandise or are not related to the growth, production, manufacture or assembly of the merchandise, such as administrative salaries, casualty and liability insurance, advertising and sales staff's salaries, commissions or expenses.

Certificate of Origin Form A

The United Nations Conference on Trade and Development (UNCTAD) Certificate of Origin Form A is used as documentary evidence to support duty-free and reduced-rate claims for Israeli articles covered by a formal entry. It does not have to be produced at the time of entry, however, unless so requested by the Customs Service. The Form A can be obtained from the Israeli authorizing issuing authority, the commercial printers of this form listed or shown on page 24 of this booklet or the UNCTAD address on the same page.

Informal Entries

The Form A is not required for commercial or non-commercial shipments covered by an informal entry. However, the district director may require such other evidence of the country of origin as deemed necessary. With regard to merchandise accompanying the traveler, it should be noted that in order to avoid delays to passengers, the inspecting Customs officer will extend Israeli duty-free or reduced rate treatment to all eligible articles when satisfied, from the facts available, that the merchandise concerned is a product of Israel. A Form A is not required for the merchandise.

Sources of Additional Information

Address any questions you may have about the administrative or operational aspects of the FTA to the Director, Office of Trade Operations, U.S. Customs Service, Washington, D.C. 20229. Requests for information concerning policy issues related to the FTA should be directed to the Chairman, Trade Policy Staff Subcommittee, Office of U.S. Trade Representative, 600 17th St., N.W., Washington, D.C. 20506.

16 compact of free association

The Compact of Free Association (FAS) is a program providing for the duty-free entry of merchandise from designated freely associated states of the United States. This program was established by Presidential Proclamation 60 30 of September 28, 1989, Section 242, became effective on October 18, 1989, and has no termination date.

Beneficiary Countries

The following freely associated states have been designated as beneficiary countries for purposes of the FAS: Marshall Islands
Federated States of Micronesia

Eligible Items

The duty-free treatment is applied to most products from the designated beneficiaries. For commercial shipments requiring formal entry, a claim for duty-free status is made by placing the letter "Z" next to the eligible subheading. The following merchandise is excluded from the duty-free exemption:

1. Textile and apparel articles which are subject to textile agreements.

2. Footwear, handbags, luggage, flat goods, work gloves, and leather wearing apparel which were not eligible for GSP treatment, discussed in Chapter 13, on April 1,1984.

3. Watches, clocks, and timing apparatus of Chapter 91 of the Harmonized Tariff Schedule (except such articles incorporating an optoelectronic display and no other type of display).

4. Buttons of subheading 9606.21.40 or 9606.29.20 of the Harmonized Tariff Schedule.

Rules of Origin

Merchandise will be eligible for FAS duty-free treatment only if the following conditions are met:

1. It must be the growth, product, or manufacture of the freely associated state.

2. The merchandise must be imported directly from the freely associated state into the customs territory of the United States.

3. At least 35 percent of the appraised value of the article imported into the United States must consist of the cost or value of materials produced in the beneficiary country and/or the direct costs of processing operations performed in the beneficiary country. In addition, the cost or value of materials produced in the customs territory of the United States may be counted toward the 35 percent value-added requirement, but only to a maximum of 15 percent of the appraised value of the imported article. The cost or value of the materials imported into the freely associated state from a non-beneficiary country may be included in calculating the 35 percent value-added requirement for an eligible article if the materials are first substantially transformed into new and different articles of commerce and are then used as constituent materials in the production of the eligible product.

Sources of Additional Information

Address any questions you may have about the administrative or operational aspects of the FAS to the director of the port or district where the merchandise will be entered or to the Director, Office of Trade Operations, U.S. Customs Service, Washington, D.C. 20229.

17 antidumping and countervailing duties

Antidumping duties (ADs) are assessed on imported merchandise of a class or kind that is sold to purchasers in the United States at a price less than the fair market value. Fair market value of merchandise is the price at which it is normally sold in the manufacturer's home market.

Countervailing duties (CVDs) are assessed to counter the effects of subsidies provided by foreign governments to merchandise that is exported to the United States. These subsidies cause the price of such merchandise to be artificially low, which causes economic "injury" to U.S. manufacturers.

The Department of Commerce, the International Trade Commission, and the U.S. Customs Service all play a part in enforcing antidumping and countervailing duty laws. The Department of Commerce is responsible for the overall administration of AD and CVD laws and for investigating allegations of dumping or foreign subsidization of imports. If warranted by the investigation, the Commerce Department also establishes the duty to be imposed on the merchandise. The ITC determines whether injury to industry has occurred, is likely to occur, or whether an industry may be hampered in its startup efforts as a result of alleged dumping or subsidies. The Customs Service assesses ADs and CVDs once the rates have been established and the ITC has made the necessary determinations.

Establishing and assessing both kinds of duties occurs during the following processes:

Investigation. AD or CVD investigations are typically initiated when a domestic industry files a petition with the Department of Commerce or when another interested party—an industry association, for example—alleges unfair competition by foreign manufacturers. Upon receipt of the petition, the Department of Commerce investigates the merits of the allegations to determine whether dumping or unfair subsidization has indeed occurred. The ITC, meanwhile, investigates whether there is reasonable indication that U.S. industries are, or are likely to be, harmed by the alleged dumping or subsidies. Results of these investigations are published in the Federal Register.

The Department of Commerce then calculates the difference between prices at which the merchandise in question is being sold in the United States and its fair market value. On the basis of such calculations, Commerce directs the Customs Service to: (1) assess cash deposits or require bonds on imports of the merchandise to cover possible AD or CVD duty liability, and (2) suspend liquidation of the entries until the Department has determined whether dumping or subsidization has occurred and has calculated the proper dumping or countervailing margins.

Completing the Investigation. When the Department of Commerce and, if applicable, the ITC have completed their investigations and determined that dumping or subsidization has occurred, Commerce will publish an Antidumping or Countervailing Duty Order, which will be announced in the Federal Register. At this point, Commerce will generally direct the Customs Service to collect only cash deposits. Bonding is no longer permitted.

Administrative Review/Final Settlement. Each year, on the anniversary of the final determination of dumping or subsidization, the Department of Commerce must, by law, perform an administrative review of the AD or CVD case if requested by interested parties to determine whether duty rates in effect for that first-year period are correct. Commerce publishes the results of this review in the Federal Register. At the one-year anniversary or completion of the administrative review, Commerce will direct Customs to liquidate the entries for the affected period. Customs will then review the entries and, if called for, make refunds to the importer or assess whatever additional duties may be owed.

18 drawback—refunds of duties

Definition

Drawback is a refund of 99% of all ordinary Customs duties and internal revenue taxes. Drawback was initially authorized by the first tariff act of the United States in 1789. Since then it has been a part of the law, although from time to time the conditions under which it is payable have changed. For example, as a result of the Omnibus Trade & Competitiveness Act of 1988, antidumping and countervailing duties are not refundable on a drawback claim.

Purpose

The rationale for drawback has always been to encourage American commerce or manufacturing, or both. It permits the American manufacturer to compete in foreign markets without the handicap of including in his costs, and consequently in his sales price, the duty paid on imported merchandise.

The types of drawback are authorized under Title 19, United States Code, Section 1313, and implemented by Title 19, Code of Federal Regulations, Part 191.

Two Types

There are two types of manufacturing drawback:

Direct identification drawback which provides a refund of duties paid on imported merchandise that is partially or totally used in the manufacture of an exported article. Identification of the imported merchandise from import to export is required by proper record-keeping procedures. The imported merchandise must be used in the manufacturing process and exported within 5 years from date of importation of merchandise (19 U.S.C. 1313(a)).

Substitution drawback provides for a refund of duties paid on designated imported merchandise upon exportation of articles manufactured or produced with use of substituted domestic or imported merchandise that is of the same kind and quality as the designated imported merchandise. Same kind and quality means merchandise that is interchangeable in a specific manufacturing process. The imported materials must be used in a manufacturing process within 3 years after receipt by manufacturer, the domestic material of same kind and quality as imported materials must be used in manufacturing process within 3 years of receipt of the imported material and the exported products must be manufactured within 3 years after receipt of imported material by manufacturer, and exported within 5 years of date of importation of designated material (19 U.S.C. 1313(b)).

Another type is same condition drawback (19 U.S.C. 1313(j)).

Duties are refunded on imported material which is subsequently exported in the same condition as when imported, or when destroyed under Customs supervision. The material must not have been used within the U.S. However, incidental operations such as testing, cleaning, inspecting and repacking are permitted. The materials must be exported or destroyed within 3 years of date of importation.

Substitution same condition drawback allows claimants to file for drawback on imported material even if the imported material is not the exact material which is exported. However, exported material must be fungible with the designated material. Fungible merchandise is merchandise which is for commercial purposes identical and interchangeable in all situations.

Rejected Merchandise

A 99 percent refund of duties is also allowed for any imported merchandise found not to conform to sample or specification, or shipped without the consent of the consignee, if returned to Customs custody within 90 days of its release (unless an extension is granted) for examination and exportation under Customs supervision. Although the foregoing "rejected merchandise" provision may still be used, the same refund may, in many cases, also be made when the merchandise is exported within 3 years of importation in the same condition as imported. Rejected merchandise must be exported and cannot be destroyed in lieu of such exportation.

Questions relating to legal aspects of drawback should be addressed to: Chief, Drawback Section, Office of Trade Operations, U.S. Customs Service, 1301 Constitution Avenue, N.W., Washington, D.C. 20229.

19 classification—liquidation

Classification

Classification and, when ad valorem rates of duty are applicable, appraisement are the two most important factors affecting dutiable status. Classifications and valuations, whether or not they are pertinent because an ad valorem rate of duty applies, must be provided by commercial importers when an entry is filed. In addition, classifications under the statistical suffixes of the tariff schedules must also be furnished even though this information is not pertinent to dutiable status. Accordingly, classification is initially the responsibility of an importer, customs broker or other person preparing the entry papers.

Familiarity with the organization of the Harmonized Tariff Schedule of the United States facilitates the classification process. (See Chapter 9 of this booklet relating to dutiable status.) The tariff schedule is divided into various sections and chapters dealing separately with merchandise in broad product categories. These categories, for example, separately cover animal products, vegetable products, products of various basic materials such as wood, textiles, plastics, rubber, and steel and other metal products in various stages of manufacture. Other sections encompass chemicals, machinery and electrical equipment, and other specified or non-enumerated products. The last section, Section XXII, covers certain exceptions from duty and special statutory provisions.

In Sections I through XXI, products are classifiable (1) under items or descriptions which name them, known as an *eo nomine* provision; (2) under provisions of general description; (3) under provisions which identify them by component material, or (4) under provisions which encompass merchandise in accordance with its actual or principal use. When two or more provisions seem to cover the same merchandise, the prevailing provision is determined in accordance with the legal notes and the General Rules of Interpretation for the tariff schedule. Also applicable are tariff classification principles contained in administrative precedents or in the case law of the U.S. Court of International Trade (formerly the U.S. Customs Court) or the U.S. Court of Appeals for the Federal Circuit (formerly the U.S. Court of Customs and Patent Appeals.)

Liquidation

Customs officers at the port of entry or other officials acting on behalf of the district director review the classifications and valuations, as well as other required import information, for correctness or as a proper basis for appraisement, as well as for agreement of the submitted data with the merchandise actually imported. The entry summary and documentation may be accepted as submitted without any changes. In this situation, the entry is liquidated as entered. Liquidation is the point at which the Customs Service's ascertainment of the rate of duty and amount of duty becomes final for most purposes. Liquidation is accomplished by posting a notice on a public bulletin board at the customhouse. However, an importer may receive an advance notice on Customs Form 4333A "Courtesy Notice" stating when and in what amount duty will be liquidated. This form is not the liquidation, and protest rights do not accrue until the notice is posted. Time limits for protesting do not start to run until the date of posting, and a protest cannot be filed before liquidation is posted.

The Customs Service may determine that an entry cannot be liquidated as entered for one reason or another. For example, the tariff classification may not be correct or may not be acceptable because it is not consistent with an established and uniform classification practice. If the change required by this determination results in a rate of duty more favorable to an importer, the entry is liquidated accordingly and a refund of the applicable amount of the deposited estimated duties is authorized. On the other hand, a change may be necessary which imposes a higher rate of duty. For example, a claim for an exemption from duty under a free-rate provision or under a conditional exemption may be found to be insufficient for lack of the required supporting documentation. In this situation the importer will be given an advance notice of the proposed duty rate advancement and an opportunity to validate the claim for a free rate or more favorable rate of duty.

If the importer does not respond to the notice, or if the response is found to be without merit, duty is liquidated in accordance with the entry as corrected and the importer is billed for the additional duty. The port or district may find that the importer's response raises issues of such complexity that resolution by a Customs Headquarters decision through the internal advice procedure is warranted. Internal advice from Customs Headquarters may be requested by the local Customs officers on their own initiative or in response to a request by the importer.

Protests

After liquidation an importer may still pursue any claims for an adjustment or refund by filing a protest within 90 days after liquidation on Customs Form 19, 19 CFR 174. In order to apply for a Headquarters ruling, a request for further review must be filed with the protest. The same Form 19 can be used for this purpose. If filed separately, application for further review must still be filed within 90 days of liquidation. However, if a ruling on the question has previously been issued in response to a request for a decision on a prospective transaction or a request for internal advice, further review will ordinarily be denied. If a protest is denied, an importer has the right to litigate the matter by filing a summons with the U.S. Court of International Trade within 180 days after denial of the protest. The rules of the court and other applicable statutes and precedents determine the course of customs litigation.

While the Customs ascertainment of dutiable status is final for most purposes at the time of liquidation, a liquidation is not final until any protest which has been filed against it has been decided. Similarly, the administrative decision issued on a protest is not final until any litigation filed against it has become final.

Entries must be liquidated within one year of the date of entry unless the liquidation needs to be extended for another one-year period not to exceed a total of four years from the date of entry. The Customs Service will suspend liquidation of an entry when required by statute or court order. A suspension will remain in effect until the issue is resolved. Notifications of extensions and suspensions are given to importers, surety companies and customs brokers who are parties to the transaction.

20   conversion of currency

The conversion of foreign currency for Customs purposes must be made in accordance with the provisions of 31 U.S.C. 5151. This section states that Customs is to use rates of exchange determined, and certified by the Federal Reserve Bank of New York. These certified rates are based on the New York market buying rates for the foreign currencies involved.

In the case of widely used currencies, rates of exchange are certified each day. The rates certified on the first business day of each calendar quarter are used throughout the quarter except on days when fluctuations of 5 percent or greater occur, in which case the actual certified rates for those days are used. For infrequently used currencies, the Federal Reserve Bank of New York certifies rates of exchange upon request by Customs. The rates certified are only for the currencies and dates requested.

For Customs purposes, the date of exportation of the goods is the date used to determine the applicable certified rate of exchange. This remains true even though a different rate may have been used in payment of the goods. Information as to the applicable rate of exchange in converting currency for customs purposes in the case of a given shipment may be obtained from a district or port director of Customs.

21   transaction value

U.S. Customs officers are required by law to determine the value for imported merchandise. The valuation provisions of the Tariff Act of 1930 are found in section 402, as amended by the Trade Agreements Act of 1979. Pertinent portions are reproduced in the appendix.

Generally, the customs value of all merchandise exported to the United States will be the transaction value for the goods. If the transaction value cannot be used, then certain secondary bases are considered. The secondary bases of value, listed in order of precedence for use, are:

Transaction value of identical merchandise,
Transaction value of similar merchandise,
Deductive value, and
Computed value.

The order of precedence of the last two values can be reversed if the importer so requests. These secondary bases are discussed in the next two chapters.

Transaction Value

The transaction value of imported merchandise is the price actually paid or payable for the merchandise when sold for exportation to the United States, plus amounts for the following items if not included in the price:

1. The packing costs incurred by the buyer.

2. Any selling commission incurred by the buyer.

3. The value of any assist.

4. Any royalty or license fee that the buyer is required to pay as a condition of the sale.

5. The proceeds, accruing to the seller, of any subsequent resale, disposal, or use of the imported merchandise.

The amounts for the above items are added only to the extent that each is not included in the price actually paid or payable and information is available to establish the accuracy of the amount. If sufficient information is not available, then the transaction value cannot be determined and the next basis of value, in order of precedence, must be considered for appraisement. A discussion of these added items follows:

Packing costs consist of the cost incurred by the buyer for all containers and coverings of whatever nature and for the labor and materials used in packing the imported merchandise, ready for export.

Any selling commission incurred by the buyer with respect to the imported merchandise constitutes part of the transaction value. Buying commissions do not. A selling commission means any commission paid to the seller's agent, who is related to or controlled by, or works for or on behalf of, the manufacturer or the seller.

The apportioned value of any assist constitutes part of the transaction value of the imported merchandise. First the value of the assist is determined; then the value is prorated to the imported merchandise.

Assists. An assist is any of the items listed below that the buyer of imported merchandise provides directly or indirectly, free of charge or at a reduced cost, for use in the production or sale of merchandise for export to the United States.

Materials, components, parts, and similar items incorporated in the imported merchandise.

Tools, dies, molds, and similar items used in producing the imported merchandise.

Merchandise consumed in producing the imported merchandise.

Engineering, development, artwork, design work, and plans and sketches that are undertaken outside the United States. "Engineering . . .," will not be treated as an assist if the service or work is (1) performed by a person domiciled within the United States, (2) performed while that person is acting as an employee or agent of the buyer of the imported merchandise, and (3) incidental to other engineering, development, artwork, design work, or plans or sketches undertaken within the United States.

Value. In determining the value of an assist, the following rules apply:

1. The value is either (a) the cost of acquiring the assist, if acquired by the importer from an unrelated seller, or (b) the cost of the assist, if produced by the importer or a person related to the importer.

2. The value includes the cost of transporting the assist to the place of production.

3. The value of assists used in producing the imported merchandise is adjusted to reflect use, repairs, modifications, or other factors affecting the value of the assists. Assists of this type include such items as tools, dies, and molds.

    For example, if the importer previously used the assist, regardless of whether he acquired or produced it, the original cost of acquisition or of production must be decreased to reflect the use. Alternatively, repairs and modifications may result in the value of the assist having to be adjusted upward.

4. In the case of engineering, development, artwork, design work, and plans and sketches undertaken elsewhere than in the United States, the value is (a) the cost of obtaining copies of the assist, if the assist is available in the public domain; (b) the cost of the purchase or lease, if the assist was bought or leased by the buyer from an unrelated person; (c) the value added outside the United States, if the assist was produced in the United States and one or more foreign countries.

So far as possible, the buyer's commercial record system will be used to determine the value of an assist, especially such assists as engineering, development, artwork, design work, and plans and sketches undertaken elsewhere than in the United States.

Apportionment. Having determined the value of an assist, the next step is to prorate that value to the imported merchandise. The apportionment is done reasonably and according to generally accepted accounting principles. By the latter is meant any generally recognized consensus or substantial authoritative support regarding the recording and measuring of assets and liabilities and changes, the disclosing of information, and the preparing of financial statements.

Royalty or license fees that a buyer must pay directly or indirectly, as a condition of the sale of the imported merchandise for exportation to the United States, will be included in the transaction value. Ultimately, whether a royalty or license fee is dutiable will depend on whether the buyer had to pay it as a condition of the sale and to whom and under what circumstances it was paid. The dutiability status will have to be decided on a case-by-case basis.

Charges for the right to reproduce the imported goods in the United States are not dutiable. This right applies only to the following types of merchandise:

> Originals or copies of artistic or scientific works.
> Originals or copies of models and industrial drawings.
> Model machines and prototypes.
> Plant and animal species.

Any proceeds resulting from the subsequent resale, disposal, or use of the imported merchandise that accrue, directly or indirectly, to the seller are dutiable. These proceeds are added to the price actually paid or payable, if not otherwise included.

The price actually paid or payable for the imported merchandise is the total payment, excluding international freight, insurance, and other c.i.f. charges, that the buyer makes to the seller. This payment may be direct or indirect. Some examples of an indirect payment are when the buyer settles all or part of a debt owed by the seller, or when the seller reduces the price on a current importation to settle a debt he owes the buyer. Such indirect payments are part of the transaction value.

However, if a buyer performs an activity on his own account, other than those which may be included in the transaction value, then the activity is not considered an indirect payment to the seller and is not part of the transaction value. This applies even though the buyer's activity might be regarded as benefiting the seller; for example, advertising.

Exclusions

The amounts to be excluded from transaction value are as follows:

1. The cost, charges, or expenses incurred for transportation, insurance, and related services incident to the international shipment of the goods from the country of exportation to the place of importation in the United States.

2. Any reasonable cost or charge incurred for:

   Constructing, erecting, assembling, maintaining, or providing technical assistance with respect to the goods after importation into the United States, or
   Transporting the goods after importation.

3. The customs duties and other Federal taxes, including any Federal excise tax for which sellers in the United States are ordinarily liable.

Note: Foreign inland freight and related charges in item 1 (see part 152, Customs Regulations), as well as items 2 and 3 above, must be identified separately.

Limitations

The transaction value of imported merchandise is the appraised value of that merchandise, provided certain limitations do not exist. If any of these limitations are present, then transaction value cannot be used as the appraised value, and the next basis of value will be considered. The limitations can be divided into four groups:

1. Restrictions on the disposition or use of the merchandise.

2. Conditions for which a value cannot be determined.

3. Proceeds of any subsequent resale, disposal or use of the merchandise, accruing to the seller, for which an appropriate adjustment to transaction value cannot be made.

4. Related-party transactions where the transaction value is not acceptable.

The term "acceptable" means that the relationship between the buyer and seller did not influence the price actually paid or payable. Examining the circumstances of the sale will help make this determination.

Alternatively, "acceptable" can also mean that the transaction value of the imported merchandise closely approximates one of the following test values, provided these values relate to merchandise exported to the United States at or about the same time as the imported merchandise:

1. The transaction value of identical merchandise or of similar merchandise in sales to unrelated buyers in the United States.

2. The deductive value or computed value for identical merchandise or similar merchandise. The test values are used for comparison only; they do not form a substitute basis of valuation.

In determining if the transaction value is close to one of the foregoing test values, an adjustment is made if the sales involved differ in:

Commercial levels,

Quantity levels,

The costs, commission, values, fees, and proceeds added to the transaction value (price paid) if not included in the price, and

The costs incurred by the seller in sales in which he and the buyer are not related that are not incurred by the seller in sales in which he and the buyer are related.

As stated, the test values are alternatives to the relationship criterion. If one of the test values is met, it is not necessary to examine the question of whether the relationship influenced the price.

22 transaction value of identical merchandise or similar merchandise

When the transaction value cannot be determined, then the customs value of the imported goods being appraised is the transaction value of identical merchandise. If merchandise identical to the imported goods cannot be found or an acceptable transaction value for such merchandise does not exist, then the customs value is the transaction value of similar merchandise. The above value would be previously accepted customs values.

Besides the data common to all three transaction values, certain factors specifically apply to the transaction value of identical merchandise or similar merchandise. These factors concern (1) the exportation date, (2) the level and quantity of sales, (3) the meaning, and (4) the order of precedence of identical merchandise and of similar merchandise.

Exportation date. The identical (similar) merchandise for which a value is being determined must have been sold for export to the United States and exported at or about the same time as the merchandise being appraised.

Sales Level/Quantity. The transaction value of identical (similar) merchandise must be based on sales of identical (similar) merchandise at the same commercial level and in substantially the same quantity as the sale of the merchandise being appraised. If no such sale exists, then sales at either a different commercial level or in different quantities, or both, can be used but must be adjusted to take account of any such difference. Any adjustment must be based on sufficient information, that is, information establishing the reasonableness and accuracy of the adjustment.

Meanings. The term "identical merchandise" means merchandise that is:

Identical in all respects to the merchandise being appraised.

Produced in the same country as the merchandise being appraised.

Produced by the same person as the merchandise being appraised.

If merchandise meeting all three criteria cannot be found, then identical merchandise is merchandise satisfying the first two criteria but produced by a different person than the producer of merchandise being appraised.

Note: Merchandise can be identical to the merchandise being appraised and still show minor differences in appearance.

Exclusion: Identical merchandise does not include merchandise that incorporates or reflects engineering, development, art work, design work, and plans and sketches provided free or at reduced cost by the buyer and undertaken in the United States.

The term "similar merchandise" means merchandise that is:

Produced in the same country and by the same person as the merchandise being appraised.

Like merchandise being appraised in characteristics and component materials.

Commercially interchangeable with the merchandise being appraised.

If merchandise meeting the foregoing criteria cannot be found, then similar merchandise is merchandise having the same country of production, like characteristics and component materials, and commercial interchangeability but produced by a different person.

In determining whether goods are similar, some of the factors to be considered are the quality of the goods, their reputation, and existence of a trademark.

Exclusion: Similar merchandise does not include merchandise that incorporates or reflects engineering, development, artwork, design work, and plans and sketches provided free or at reduced cost to the buyer and undertaken in the United States.

Order of Precedence. It is possible that two or more transaction values for identical (similar) merchandise will be determined. In such a case the lowest value will be used as the appraised value of the imported merchandise.

23 other bases: deductive and computed value

Deductive Value

If the transaction value of imported merchandise, of identical merchandise, or of similar merchandise cannot be determined, then deductive value is calculated for the merchandise being appraised. Deductive value is the next basis of appraisement at the time the entry summary is filed, to be used unless the importer designates computed value as the preferred method of appraisement. If computed value was chosen and subsequently determined not to exist for customs valuation purposes, then the basis of appraisement reverts to deductive value.

If an assist is involved in a sale, that sale cannot be used in determining deductive value. So any sale to a person who supplies an assist for use in connection with the production or sale for export of the merchandise concerned is disregarded for purposes of determining deductive value.

Basically, deductive value is the resale price in the United States after importation of the goods, with deductions for certain items. In discussing deductive value, the term "merchandise concerned" is used. The term means the merchandise being appraised, identical merchandise, or similar merchandise. Generally, the deductive value is calculated by starting with a unit price and making certain additions to and deductions from that price.

Unit Price. One of three prices constitutes the unit price in deductive value. The price used depends on when and in what condition the merchandise concerned is sold in the United States.

1. Time and Condition: The merchandise is *sold in the condition* as imported *at or about the date of importation* of the merchandise being appraised.

Price: The price used is the unit price at which the greatest aggregate quantity of the merchandise concerned is sold at or about date of importation.

2. Time and Condition: The merchandise concerned is *sold in the condition as imported but not sold at or about the date of importation* of the merchandise being appraised.

Price: The price used is the unit price at which the greatest aggregate quantity of the merchandise concerned is sold after the date of importation of the merchandise being appraised but before the close of the 90th day after the date of importation.

3. Time and Condition: The merchandise concerned is *not sold in the condition* as imported and *not sold before the close of the 90th day* after the date of importation of the merchandise being appraised.

Price: The price used is the unit price at which the greatest aggregate quantity of the merchandise being appraised, after further processing, is sold before the 180th day after the date of importation.

This third price is also known as the "further processing price" or "superdeductive."

Additions. Packing costs for the merchandise concerned are added to the price used for deductive value, provided these costs have not otherwise been included. These costs are added regardless of whether the importer or the buyer incurs the cost. Packing costs means the cost of:

1. All containers and coverings of whatever nature; and

2. Packing, whether for labor or materials, used in placing the merchandise in condition, packed ready for shipment to the United States.

Deductions. Certain items are not part of deductive value and must be deducted from the unit price. These items are as follows:

1. Commissions or Profit and General Expenses. Any commission usually paid or agreed to be paid, or the addition usually made for profit and general expenses, applicable to sales in the United States of imported merchandise that is of the same class or kind as the merchandise concerned regardless of the country of exportation.

2. Transportation/Insurance Costs. The usual and associated costs of transporting and insuring the merchandise concerned from (a) the country of exportation to the place of importation in the United States and (b) the place of importation to the place of delivery in the United States, provided these costs are not included as a general expense under the preceding item 1.

3. Customs Duties/Federal Taxes. The customs duties and other Federal taes payable on the merchandise concerned because of its importation plus any Federal excise tax on, or measured by the value of, such merchandise for which sellers in the United States are ordinarily liable.

4. Value of Further Processing. The value added by the processing of the merchandise after importation, provided sufficient information exists concerning the cost of processing. The price determined for deductive value is reduced by the value of further processing only if the third unit price (the suprdeductive) is used as deductive value.

Superdeductive. The importer has the option to ask that deductive value be based on the further processing price. If the importer makes that choice, certain facts concerning valuing the further-processing method, termed "superdeductive," must be followed.

Under the superdeductive, the merchandise concerned is not sold in the condition as imported and not sold before the close of the 90th day after the date of importation, but is sold before the 180th day after the date of importation.

Under this method, an amount equal to the value of the further processing must be deducted from the unit price in determining deductive value. The amount so deducted must be based on objective and quantifiable data concerning the cost of such work as well as any spoilage, waste or scrap derived from that work. Items such as accepted industry formulas, methods of construction, and industry practices could be used as a basis for calculating the amount to be deducted.

Generally, the superdeductive method cannot be used if the further processing destroys the identity of the goods. Such situations will be decided on a case-by-case basis for the following reasons:

1. Sometimes, even though the identity of the goods is lost, the value added by the processing can be determined accurately without unreasonable difficulty for importers or for the Customs Service.

2. In some cases, the imported goods still keep their identity after processing but form only a minor part of the goods sold in the United States. In such cases, using the superdeductive method to value the imported goods will not be justified.

The superdeductive method cannot be used if the merchandise concerned is sold in the condition as imported before the close of the 90th day after the date of importation of the merchandise being appraised.

Computed Value

The next basis of appraisement is computed value. If customs valuation cannot be based on any of the values previously discussed, then computed value is considered. This value is also the one the importer can select to precede deductive value as a basis of appraisement.

Computed value consists of the sum of the following items:

1. Materials, fabrication, and other processing used in producing the imported merchandise.

2. Profit and general expenses.

3. Any assist, if not included in items 1 and 2.

4. Packing costs.

Materials, Fabrication, and Other Processing. The cost or value of the materials, fabrication, and other processing of any kind used in producing the imported merchandise is based on (a) information provided by or on behalf of the producer and (b) the commercial accounts of the producer if the accounts are consistent with generally accepted accounting principles applied in the country of production of the goods.

Note: If the country of exportation imposes an internal tax on the materials or their disposition and refunds the tax when merchandise produced from the materials is exported, then the amount of the internal tax is not included as part of the cost or value of the materials.

Profit and General Expenses. The producer's profit and general expenses are used, provided they are consistent with the usual profit and general expenses reflected by producers in the country of exportation in sales of merchandise of the same class or kind as the imported merchandise. Some facts concerning the amount for profit and general expenses should be mentioned:

1. The amount is determined by information supplied by the producer and is based on his commercial accounts, provided such accounts are consistent with generally accepted accounting principles in the country of production.

Note: As a point of contrast, for deductive value the generally accepted accounting principles used are those in the United States, whereas in computed value the generally accepted accounting principles are those in the country of production.

2. The producer's profit and general expenses must be consistent with those usually reflected in sales of goods of the same class or kind as the imported merchandise that are made by producers in the country of exportation for export to the United States. If they are not consistent, then the amount for profit and general expenses is based on the usual profit and general expenses of such producers.

3. The amount for profit and general expenses is taken as a whole. This is the same treatment as occurs in deductive value.

Basically, a producer's profit could be low and his general expenses high, so that the total amount is consistent with that usually reflected in sales of goods of the same class or kind. In such a situation, a producer's actual profit figures, even if low, will be used provided he has valid commercial reasons to justify them and his pricing policy reflects usual pricing policies in the industry concerned.

Assists. If the value of an assist used in producing the merchandise is not included as part of the producer's materials, fabrication, other processing, or general expenses, then the prorated value of the assist will be included in computed value. It is important that the value of the assist is not included elsewhere because no component of computed value should be counted more than once in determining computed value.

Note: The value of any engineering, development, artwork, design work, and plans and sketches undertaken in the United States is included in computed value only to the extent that such value has been charged to the producer.

Packing Costs. The cost of all containers and coverings of whatever nature, and of packing, whether for labor or material, used in placing merchandise in condition and packed ready for shipment to the United States is included in computed value.

Under computed value, "merchandise of the same class or kind" must be imported from the same country as the merchandise being appraised and must be within a group or range of goods produced by a particular industry or industry sector. Whether certain merchandise is of the same class or kind as other merchandise will be determined on a case-by-case basis.

In determining usual profit and general expenses, sales for export to the United States of the narrowest group or range of merchandise that includes the merchandise being appraised will be examined, providing the necessary information can be obtained.

Note: As a point of contrast, under deductive value, "merchandise of the same class or kind" includes merchandise imported from other countries besides the country from which the merchandise being appraised was imported. Under computed value, "Merchandise of the same class or kind" is limited to merchandise imported from the same country as the merchandise being appraised.

Value If Other Values Cannot Be Determined

If none of the previous five values can be used to appraise the imported merchandise, then the customs value must be based on a value derived from one of the five previous methods, reasonably adjusted as necessary. The value so determined should be based, to the greatest extent possible, on previously determined values. Only data available in the United States will be used.

Some examples of how the other methods can be reasonably adjusted are:

1. Identical Merchandise (or Similar Merchandise):

   a. The requirement that the identical merchandise (or similar merchandise) should be exported at or about the same time as the merchandise being appraised could be flexibly interpreted.

   b. Identical imported merchandise (or similar imported merchandise) produced in a country other than the country of exportation of the merchandise being appraised could be the basis for customs valuation.

   c. Customs values of identical imported merchandise (or similar imported merchandise) already determined on the basis of deductive value and computed value could be used.

2. Deductive Method: The 90-day requirement may be administered flexibly (19 CFR 152.107(c)).

The United States customs laws require each imported article produced abroad to be marked in a conspicuous place as legibly, indelibly, and permanently as the nature of the article permits, with the English name of the country of origin, to indicate to the ultimate purchaser in the United States the name of the country in which the article was manufactured or produced. Articles which are otherwise specifically exempted from individual marking are an exception to this rule. The exceptions are discussed below.

Marking Required

If the article (or the container when the container and not the article must be marked) is not properly marked at the time of importation, a marking duty equal to 10 percent of the customs value of the article will be assessed unless the article is exported, destroyed, or properly marked under Customs supervision before the liquidation of the entry concerned.

It is not feasible to state who will be the "ultimate purchaser" in every circumstance. Broadly stated, an "ultimate purchaser" may be defined as the last person in the United States who will receive the article in the form in which it was imported. Generally, if an imported article will be used in the U.S. in manufacture, which results in an article having a name, character or usage different from that of the imported article, the manufacturer is the ultimate purchaser. If an article is to be sold at retail in its imported form, the purchaser at retail is the ultimate purchaser. A person who subjects an imported article to a process which results in a substantial transformation of the article is the ultimate purchaser, but if the process is merely a minor one which leaves the identity of the imported article intact, the processor of the article will not be regarded as the ultimate purchaser.

When an article (or its container) is required to be marked to indicate the country of origin of the article, the marking is sufficiently permanent if it will remain on the article (or its container) until it reaches the ultimate purchaser.

When an article is of a kind which is usually combined with another article subsequent to importation but before delivery to an ultimate purchaser, and the name indicating the country of origin of the article appears in a place on the article so that the name will be visible after such combining, the marking shall include, in addition to the name of the country of origin, words or symbols which clearly show that the origin indicated is that of the imported article only and not that of any other article with which the imported article may be combined after importation, For example, if marked bottles, drums, or other containers are imported empty, to be filled in the United States, they shall be marked with such words as "Bottle (or drum or container) made in (name of country)." Labels and similar articles so marked that the name of the country of origin of the article is visible after it is affixed to another article in this country shall be marked with additional descriptive words such as "label made (or printed) in (name of country)" or words of similar import.

In any case in which the words "United States," or "American" or the letters "U.S.A.," any variation of such words or letters, or the name of any city or locality in the United States, or the name of any foreign country or locality in which the article was manufactured or produced, appear on an imported article or container, there shall appear, legibly and permanently, in close proximity to such words, letters or name, the name of the country of origin preceded by "Made in," "Product of," or other words of similar meaning.

If marked articles are to be repacked in the United States after release from Customs custody, importers must certify on entry that they will not obscure the marking on properly marked articles if the article is repacked or that they will mark the repacked container. If the importers do not repack, but resell to repackers, importers must notify the repackers of the marking requirements. Failure to comply with the certification requirements may subject importers to penalties and/or additional duties.

Marking Not Required

The following articles and classes or kinds of articles are not required to be marked to indicate the country of their origin, i.e., the country in which they were grown, manufactured, or produced. However, the outermost containers in which these articles ordinarily reach the ultimate purchaser in the United States must be marked to indicate the English name of the country of origin of the articles.

Art, works of.
Articles classified subheads 9810.00.15, 9810.00.25, 9810.00.40, and 9810.00.45, HTSUS.
Articles entered in good faith as antiques and rejected as unauthentic.
Bagging, waste.
Bags, jute.
Bands, steel.
Beads, unstrung.
Bearings, ball, $^5/_8$-inch or less in diameter.
Blanks, metal, to be plated.
Bodies, harvest hat.
Bolts, nuts, and washers.
Briarwood, in blocks.
Briquettes, coal or coke.
Buckles, 1 inch or less in greatest dimension.
Burlap.
Buttons.
Cards, playing.
Cellophane and celluloid in sheets, bands, or strips.
Chemicals, drugs, medicinal, and similar substances, when imported in capsules, pills, tablets, lozenges, or troches.
Cigars and cigarettes.
Covers, straw bottle.
Dies, diamond wire, unmounted.
Dowels, wooden.
Effects, theatrical.
Eggs.
Feathers.
Firewood.
Flooring, not further manufactured than planed, tongued and grooved.
Flowers, artificial, except bunches.
Flowers, cut.
Glass, cut to shape and size for use in clocks, hand pocket, and purse mirrors, and other glass of similar shapes and sizes, not including lenses or watch crystals.
Glides, furniture, except glides with prongs.
Hairnets.
Hides, raw.
Hooks, fish (except snelled fish hooks).
Hoops (wood), barrel.
Laths.
Leather, except finished.
Livestock.
Lumber, sawed.
Metal bars except concrete reinforcement bars, billets, blocks, blooms, ingots, pigs, plates, sheets, except galvanized sheets, shafting, slabs, and metal in similar forms.

Mica not further manufactured than cut or stamped to dimensions, shape, or form.
Monuments.
Nails, spikes, and staples.
Natural products, such as vegetables, fruit, nuts, berries, and live or dead animals, fish and birds; all the foregoing which are in their natural state or not advanced in any manner further than is necessary for their safe transportation.
Nets, bottle wire.
Paper, newsprint.
Paper, stencil.
Paper, stock.
Parchment and vellum.
Parts for machines imported from same country as parts.
Pickets (wood).
Pins, tuning.
Plants, shrubs, and other nursery stock.
Plugs, tie.
Poles, bamboo.
Posts (wood), fence.
Pulpwood.
Rags (including wiping rags).
Rails, joint bars, and tie plates of steel.
Ribbon.
Rivets.
Rope, including wire rope, cordage, cords, twines, threads, and yarns.
Scrap and waste.
Screws.
Shims, track.
Shingles (wood), bundles of, except bundles of red-cedar shingles.
Skins, fur, dressed or dyed.
Skins, raw fur.
Sponges.
Springs, watch.
Stamps, postage and revenue, and Government stamped envelopes and postal cards bearing no printing other than the official import thereon.
Staves (wood), barrel.
Steel, hoop.
Sugar, maple.
Ties (wood), railroad.
Tiles, not over 1 inch in greatest dimension.
Timbers, sawed.
Tips, penholder.
Trees, Christmas.
Weights, analytical and precision, in sets.
Wicking, candle.
Wire, except barbed.

Unless an article being shipped to the United States is specifically named in the foregoing list, it would be advisable for an exporter to obtain advice from U.S. Customs before concluding that it is exempted from marking.

If articles on the foregoing list are repacked in the United States, the new packages must be labeled to indicate the country of origin of the articles contained therein. Importers must certify on entry that, if they repackage, they will properly mark the repackaged containers; if they do not repackage, but resell to repackagers, notification of the marking requirements will be given to such repackagers. Failure to comply with the certification requirements may subject importers to penalties and marking duties.

Other Exceptions   The following classes of articles are excepted from the country of origin marking requirements. (The usual container in which one of these articles is imported will also be excepted from marking.):

1. An article imported for use by the importer and not intended for sale in its imported or any other form.

2. An article which is to be processed in the United States by the importer or for his account otherwise than for the purpose of concealing the origin of the article and in such manner that any mark of origin would necessarily be obliterated, destroyed, or permanently concealed.

3. An article with respect to which an ultimate purchaser in the United States, by reason of the character of the article, or by reason of the circumstances of its importation, must necessarily know the country of origin even though the article is not marked to indicate its origin. The clearest application of this exemption is when the contract between the ultimate purchaser in the United States and the supplier abroad insures that the order will be filled only with articles grown, manufactured, or produced in a named country.

The following classes of articles are also excepted from marking to indicate the country of their origin:

1. Articles that are incapable of being marked.

2. Articles that cannot be marked prior to shipment to the United States without injury.

3. Articles that cannot be marked prior to shipment to the United States, except at an expense economically prohibitive of their importation.

4. Articles for which the marking of the containers will reasonably indicate the origin of the articles.

5. Crude substances.

6. Articles produced more than 20 years prior to their importation into the United States.

7. Articles entered or withdrawn from warehouse for immediate exportation or for transportation and exportation.

Although such articles are exempted from marking to indicate the country of their origin, the outermost containers in which the articles will ordinarily reach the ultimate purchaser in the United States must be marked to show the country of origin of such articles.

When the marking of the container of an article will reasonably indicate the country of origin of the article, the article itself may be exempt from such marking. This exemption applies only when the articles will reach the ultimate purchaser in an unopened container. For example, articles which reach the retail purchaser in sealed containers marked clearly to indicate the country of origin come within this exception. Materials to be used in building or manufacture by the builder or manufacturer who will receive the materials in unopened cases likewise come within the exemption.

8. Products of American fisheries that are free of duty.

9. Products of possessions of the United States.

10. Products of the United States exported and returned.

11. Articles valued at not more than $5 that are passed without entry.

25   special marking requirements

The Country of Origin marking requirements are separate and apart from any special marking or labeling required on specific products by other agencies. It is recommended that the specific agency be contacted for any special marking or labeling requirements.

Special marking or labeling requirements for wood, textile, and fur products are set forth in this chapter and for containers of alcoholic beverages, Chapter 29.

Certain articles are subject to special country of origin marking requirements: Iron and steel pipe and pipe fittings, manhole rings, frames, or covers, and compressed gas cylinders, must generally be marked by one of four methods: die-stamped, cast-in-mold lettering, etching (acid or electrolytic) or engraving. In addition, none of the exceptions from marking discussed above are applicable to iron and steel pipe and pipe fittings.

The following articles, and parts thereof, shall be marked legibly and conspicuously to indicate their origin by die-stamping, cast-in-the-mold lettering, etching (acid or electrolytic), engraving, or by means of metal plates which bear the prescribed marking and which are securely attached to the article in a conspicuous place by welding, screws, or rivets:

Knives, clippers, shears, safety razors, surgical instruments, scientific and laboratory instruments, pliers, pincers and vacuum containers.

Watch movements are required to be marked on one or more of the bridges or top plates to show (1) the name of the country of manufacture, (2) the name of the manufacturer or purchaser, and (3) in words, the number of jewels, if any, serving a mechanical purpose as frictional bearings.

Clock movements shall be marked on the most visible part of the front or back plate to show (1) the name of the country of manufacture, (2) the name of the manufacturer or purchaser, and (3) the number of jewels, if any.

Watch cases shall be marked on the inside or outside of the back cover to show (1) the name of the country of manufacture, and (2) the name of the manufacturer or purchaser.

Clock cases and other cases provided for in Chapter 91, HTSUS, are required to be marked on the most visible part of the outside of the back to show the name of the country of manufacture.

The terms "watch movement" and "clock movement" refer to devices regulated by a balance wheel and hairspring, quartz crystal, or any other system capable of determining intervals of time, with a display or system to which a mechanical display can be incorporated. "Watch movements" include those devices which do not exceed 12 mm in thickness and 50 mm in width, length, or diameter; "clock movements" include those devices which do not meet the watch movement dimensional specifications. The term "cases" embraces inner and outer cases, containers, and housings for movements, together with parts or pieces, such as, but not limited to, rings, feet, posts, bases, and outer frames, and any auxiliary or incidental features, which (with appropriate movements) serve to complete the watches, clocks, time switches, and other apparatus provided for in Chapter 91, HTSUS.

Articles required to be marked in accordance with the special marking requirements in Chapter 91 must be conspicuously and indelibly marked by cutting, die-sinking, engraving, or stamping. Articles required to be so marked shall be denied entry unless marked in exact conformity with these requirements.

Movements with opto-electronic display only and cases designed for use therewith, whether entered as separate articles or as components of assembled watches or clocks, are not subject to the special marking requirements. These items need only to be marked with the marking requirements of 19 USC 1304.

Parts of any of the foregoing not including those above mentioned.

In addition to the special marking requirements set forth above, all watches of foreign origin must comply with the usual country of origin marking requirements. Customs considers the country of origin of watches to be the country of manufacture of the watch movement. The name of this country should appear either on the outside back cover or on the face of the dial.

26 marking—false impression

Section 42 of the Trade-Mark Act of 1946 (15 U.S.C. 1124) provides, among other things, that no imported article of foreign origin which bears a name or mark calculated to induce the public to believe that it was manufactured in the United States, or in any foreign country or locality other than the country or locality in which it was in fact manufactured, shall be admitted to entry at any customhouse in the United States.

In many cases, the words "United States," the letters "U.S.A.," or the name of any city or locality in the United States appearing on an imported article of foreign origin, or on the containers thereof, are considered to be calculated to induce the public to believe that the article was manufactured in the United States unless the name to indicate the country of origin appears in close proximity to the name which indicates a domestic origin.

An imported article bearing a name or mark prohibited by Section 42 of the Trade-Mark Act is subject to seizure and forfeiture. However, upon the filing of a petition by the importer prior to final disposition of the article, the district or port director of Customs may release it upon the condition that the prohibited marking be removed or obliterated or that the article and containers be properly marked; or the district or port director may permit the article to be exported or destroyed under Customs supervision and without expense to the Government.

Section 43 of the Trade-Mark Act of 1946 (15 U.S.C. 1125) prohibits the entry of goods marked or labeled with a false designation of origin or with any false description or representation, including words or other symbols tending to falsely describe or represent the same.

27   user fees

Customs user fees were established by the Consolidated Omnibus Budget Reconciliation Act of 1985. This legislation was expanded in 1986 to include a merchandise processing fee. Also in 1986, Congress enacted the Water Resources Development Act, which authorized the Customs Service to collect a harbor maintenance fee for the Army Corps of Engineers. Further legislation has extended the User Fee Program until 1995.

The merchandise processing fee sets a fee schedule for formal entries (generally, those valued over $1250) at a minimum of $21 per entry and a maximum of $400 per entry, with an ad valorem rate of 0.17 percent. The fee for informal entries (those valued under $1250) is $2 for automated entries, $5 for manual entries not prepared by Customs, and $8 for manual entries prepared by Customs.

The harbor maintenance fee is an ad valorem fee assessed on cargo imports and admissions into foreign trade zones. The fee is 0.125 percent of the value of the cargo and is paid quarterly, except for imports which are paid at the time of entry. Customs deposits the harbor maintenance fee collections into the Harbor Maintenance Trust Fund. The funds are made available, subject to appropriation, to the Army Corps of Engineers for the improvement and maintenance of United States ports and harbors.

The importation of certain classes of merchandise may be prohibited or restricted to protect the economy and security of the United States, to safeguard consumer health and well-being, and to preserve domestic plant and animal life. Some commodities are also subject to an import quota or a restraint under bilateral trade agreements and arrangements.

Many of these prohibitions and restrictions on importations are subject, in addition to Customs requirements, to the laws and regulations administered by other United States Government agencies with which Customs cooperates in enforcement. These laws and regulations may, for example, prohibit entry; limit entry to certain ports; restrict routing, storage, or use; or require treatment, labeling, or processing as a condition of release. Customs clearance is given only if these various additional requirements are met. This applies to all types of importations, including those made by mail and those placed in foreign-trade zones.

The foreign exporter should make certain that the United States importer has provided proper information to (1) permit the submission of necessary information concerning packing, labeling. etc., and (2) that necessary arrangements have been made by the importer for entry of the merchandise into the United States.

It may be impracticable to list all articles specifically; however, various classes of articles are discussed below. Foreign exporters and U.S. importers should consult the agency mentioned for detailed information and guidance, as well as for any changes to the laws and regulations under which the commodities are controlled.

Agricultural Commodities

1. Cheese, Milk, and Dairy Products. Cheese and cheese products are subject to requirements of the Food and Drug Administration and the Department of Agriculture. Most importations of cheese require an import license and are subject to quotas administered by the Department of Agriculture, Foreign Agricultural Service, Washington, D.C. 20250 (see Chapter 31).

The importation of milk and cream is subject to requirements of the Food, Drug and Cosmetic Act and the Import Milk Act. These products may be imported only by holders of permits from the Department of Health and Human Services, Food and Drug Administration, Rockville, Md. 20857, and the Department of Agriculture.

2. Fruits, Vegetables, and Nuts. Certain agricultural commodities (including fresh tomatoes, avocados, mangoes, limes, oranges, grapefruit, green peppers, Irish potatoes, cucumbers, eggplants, dry onions, walnuts and filberts, processed dates, prunes, raisins, and olives in tins) must meet United States import requirements relating to grade, size, quality, and maturity (7 U.S.C. 608(e)). These commodities are inspected and an inspection certificate must be issued by the Food Safety and Quality Service of the Department of Agriculture to indicate import compliance. Inquiries on general requirements should be made to the Agricultural Marketing Service of the Department of Agriculture, Washington, D.C. 20250. Additional restrictions may be imposed by the Animal and Plant Health Inspection Service of that department, Washington, D.C. 20782, under the Plant Quarantine Act and by the Food and Drug Administration under the Federal Food, Drug and Cosmetic Act.

3. Insects. Insects in a live state which are injurious to cultivated crops (including vegetables, field crops, bush fruit, and orchard, forest, or shade trees) and the eggs, pupae, or larvae of such insects are prohibited importation, except for scientific purposes under regulations prescribed by the Secretary of Agriculture.

All packages containing live insects or their eggs, pupae, or larvae, which are not injurious to crops or trees, are permitted entry into the United States only if covered by a permit issued by the Animal and Plant Health Inspection Service of the Department of Agriculture and are not prohibited by the U.S. Fish and Wildlife Service.

4. Livestock and Animals. Inspection and quarantine requirements of the Animal and Plant Health Inspection Service must be met for the importation of (1) all cloven-hoofed animals (ruminants), such as cattle, sheep, deer, antelope, camels, giraffes; (2) swine including the various varieties of wild hogs and the meat from such animals; (3) horses, asses, mules, and zebras; (4) animal by-products, such as untanned hides, wool, hair, bones, bone meal, blood meal, animal casings, glands, organs, extracts or secretions of ruminants and swine; and (5) hay and straw. A permit for importation must be obtained from that agency before shipping from the country of origin. An exception is made in the case of

Canada and certain northern states of Mexico. Importations from any country where rinderpest or foot-and-mouth disease exists are prohibited; also, hay and straw packing materials from these countries are not eligible for entry into the United States. Entry of animals is restricted to certain ports which are designated as quarantine stations.

5. Meat and Meat Products. All commercial shipments of meat and meat food products (derived from cattle, sheep, swine, goats, and horses) offered for entry into the United States are subject to the regulations of the Department of Agriculture and must be inspected by the Animal and Plant Health Inspection Service and the Food Safety and Inspection Service of that department prior to release by U.S. Customs. Meat products from other sources (including, but not limited to wild game) are subject to the provisions of the Federal Food, Drug, and Cosmetic Act, enforced by the Food and Drug Administration.

6. Plant and Plant Products. The importation of plants and plant products is subject to regulations of the Department of Agriculture and may be restricted or prohibited. Plants and plant products include fruits, vegetables, plants, nursery stock, bulbs, roots, seeds, certain fibers including cotton and broom-corn, cut flowers, sugarcane, certain cereals, elm logs and elm lumber with bark attached. Import permits are required. Further information should be obtained from the Animal and Plant Health Inspection Service. Also certain endangered species of plants may be prohibited or require permits or certificates. The Food and Drug Administration also regulates plant and plant products, particularly fruits and vegetables.

7. Poultry and Poultry Products. Poultry, live, dressed, or canned; eggs, including eggs for hatching; and egg products are subject to the requirements and regulations of the Animal and Plant Health Inspection Service and the Food Safety and Quality Service of the Department of Agriculture. Permits are required, as well as special marking and labeling; and, in some cases, foreign inspection certification. The term "poultry" is defined as any live or slaughtered domesticated bird, e.g., chickens, turkeys, ducks, geese, or guineas. Other birds (e.g., quail and migratory birds) as well as certain egg products are subject to the provisions of the Federal Food, Drug, and Cosmetic Act, enforced by the Food and Drug Administration. Inquiry should also be made to the Fish and Wildlife Service, Washington, DC 20240, about their requirements, restrictions, and prohibitions.

8. Seeds. The importation into the United States of agricultural and vegetable seeds and screenings is governed by the provisions of the Federal Seed Act of 1939 and regulations of the Agricultural Marketing Service, Department of Agriculture. Shipments are detained pending the drawing and testing of samples.

Arms, Ammunition, Radioactive Materials

9. Arms, Ammunition, Explosives, and Implements of War. These items are prohibited importation except when a license is issued by the Bureau of Alcohol, Tobacco and Firearms of the Department of the Treasury, Washington, D.C. 20226, (202) 927-7920, or the importation is in compliance with the regulations of that department. The temporary importation, in-transit movement, and exportation of arms and ammunition is prohibited unless a license is issued by the Office of Munitions Control, Department of State, Washington, D.C. 20520.

10. Radioactive Materials and Nuclear Reactors. Many radioisotopes, all forms of uranium, thorium, and plutonium, and all nuclear reactors imported into the United States are subject to the regulations of the Nuclear Regulatory Commission in addition to import regulations imposed by any other agency of the United States. Authority to import these commodities or articles containing these commodities is granted by the Nuclear Regulatory Commission, Washington D.C. 20520.

Radioisotopes and radioactive sources intended for medical use are subject to the provisions of the Federal Food, Drug, and Cosmetic Act, enforced by the Food and Drug Administration.

In order to comply with the Nuclear Regulatory Commission requirements, the importer must be aware of the identity and amount of any NRC-controlled radioisotopes, or uranium, thorium, and plutonium, and of any nuclear reactor being imported into the United States. To assure passage through Customs, the importer must demonstrate to U.S. Customs the Nuclear Regulatory Commission authority under which the controlled commodity is being imported. The authority cited may be the number of a specific or general license, or the specific section of the Nuclear Regulatory Commission regulations which establishes a general license or grants an exemption to the regulations. The foreign exporter may save time for the prospective importer by furnishing him complete information concerning the presence of NRC-controlled commodities in U.S. importation.

11. Household appliances. The Energy Policy and Conservation Act, as amended, calls for energy efficiency standards for household consumer appliances and for labeling them to indicate expected energy or secretions of consumption. The Department of Energy, Consumer Products Efficiency Branch, Washington, D.C. 20585, is responsible for test procedures and energy performance standards. The Federal Trade Commission, Division of Energy and Product Information, Washington, D.C. 20580, regulates the labeling of these appliances. The Act covers the following consumer products: (1) refrigerators and refrigerator-freezers; (2) freezers; (3) dishwashers; (4) clothes dryers; (5) water heaters; (6) room air conditioners; (7) home heating equipment, not including furnaces; (8) television sets; (9) kitchen ranges and ovens; (10) clothes washers; (11) humidifiers and dehumidifiers; (12) central air conditioners; (13) furnaces; (14) certain other types of household consumer appliances, as appropriate.

Importations of these products must comply with the applicable Department of Energy and Federal Trade Commission requirements. Importers should contact these agencies for requirements which will be in effect at the time of anticipated shipment. It should be noted that not all appliances are covered by requirements of both agencies.

Any consumer product offered for importation will be refused admission if the product fails to comply with an applicable consumer product safety rule, specified labeling or certification requirements, or is determined to be a hazardous product or contain a product defect which constitutes a substantial product hazard.

12. Flammable Fabrics. Any article of wearing apparel or interior furnishing, or any fabric or related material which is intended for use or which may be used in wearing apparel or interior furnishings cannot be imported into the United States if it fails to conform to an applicable flammability standard issued under section 4 of the Flammable Fabrics Act. This Act is administered by the U.S. Consumer Product Safety Commission, Washington, D.C. 20207. Certain products can be imported into the United States as provided in Section 11(c) of the Act for the purpose of finishing or processing to render such products not so highly flammable as to be dangerous when worn by individuals, provided that the exporter states on the invoice or other paper relating to the shipment that the shipment is being made for that purpose. The provisions of the Flammable Fabrics Act apply to products manufactured in the United States, as well as to imported products.

13. Radiation Producing Products, Including Sonic Radiation. Television receivers, cold-cathode gas discharge tubes, microwave ovens, cabinet and diagnostic X-ray equipment and devices, laser products, ultrasound generating equipment, sunlamps, and other electronic products for which there are radiation performance standards are subject to the Radiation Control for Health and Safety Act of 1968. An electronic product imported for sale or use in the United States for which there is a radiation performance standard may be imported only if there is filed with each importation an importer's entry notice (Form FD 701) and an electronic product declaration (Form FD 2877) which are issued by the Food and Drug Administration, National Center for Devices and Radiological Health, 1390 Piccard Dr., Rockville, MD 20850.

The declaration must describe the compliance status of the product. The importer must affirm that the product either was (1) manufactured prior to the effective date of the applicable Federal standard; or (2) complies with the standard and has a label affixed by the manufacturer certifying compliance; or (3) does not comply with the standard but is being imported only for purposes of research, investigation, study, demonstration, or training; or (4) does not now comply with the standard but will be brought into compliance. The provisions of the Radiation Control for Health and Safety Act apply to electronic products manufactured in the United States, as well as to imported products.

14. Radio Frequency Devices. Radios, tape recorders, stereos, televisions, citizen band radios or combinations thereof, and other radio frequency devices are subject to radio emission standards of the Federal Communications Commission, Washington D.C. 20554, (202) 632-6345, under the Communications act of 1934, as amended. Importations of such products may be accompanied by an FCC declaration (FCC 740) certifying that the imported model or device is in conformity with, will be brought into conformity, or is exempt from the Federal Communications Commission requirements.

15. Foods, Cosmetics, Etc. The importation into the United States of food, beverages, drugs, devices, and cosmetics is governed by the provisions of the Federal Food, Drug, and Cosmetic Act, which is administered by the Food and Drug Administration of the Department of Health and Human Services, Rockville, Md. 20857. That Act prohibits the importation of articles that are adulterated or misbranded including products that are defective, unsafe, filthy, or produced under unsanitary conditions. The term "misbranded" includes statements, designs, or pictures in labeling that are false or misleading and failure to provide required information in labeling.

Imported products regulated by the Food and Drug Administration are subject to inspection at the time of entry. Shipments found not to comply with the laws and regulations are subject to detention. They must be brought into compliance, destroyed, or re-exported. At the discretion of the Food and Drug Administration, an importer may be permitted to bring a nonconforming importation into compliance if it is possible to do so. Any sorting, reprocessing, or relabeling must be supervised by the Food and Drug Administration at the expense of the importer.

Various imported foods such as confectionery, dairy products, poultry, eggs and egg products, meats, fruits, nuts, and vegetables are also subject to requirements of other agencies as discussed in this booklet. Seafoods are also subject to the requirements of the National Marine Fisheries Service of the Department of Commerce, Washington, D.C. 20910.

16. Biological Drugs. The manufacture and importation of biological products for human consumption are regulated under the Public Health Service Act. Domestic and foreign manufacturers of such products must obtain a license for both the manufacturing establishment and the product intended to be produced or imported. Additional information may be obtained from the Food and Drug Administration, Department of Health and Human Services, Rockville, Md. 20857.

Biological drugs for animals are regulated under the Virus Serum Toxin Act administered by the Department of Agriculture. The importation of viruses, serums, toxins and analogous products, and organisms and vectors for use in the treatment of domestic animals is prohibited unless the importer holds a permit from the Department of Agriculture covering the specific product. These importations are also subject to special labeling requirements.

17. Biological Materials and Vectors. The importation into the United States for sale, barter, or exchange of any virus, therapeutic serum, toxin, antitoxin, or analogous products, or arsphenamine or its derivatives (or any other trivalent organic arsenic compound), except materials to be used in research experiments, applicable to the prevention, treatment, or cure of diseases or injuries of man is prohibited unless these products have been propagated or prepared at an establishment holding an unsuspended and unrevoked license for such manufacturing issued by the Secretary, Department of Health and Human Services. Samples of the licensed product must accompany each importation for forwarding by the port director of Customs at the port of entry to the Director, National Center for Biologics Evaluation and Research, 5600 Fishers Lane, Rockville, MD 20857.

A permit from the U.S. Public Health Service, Atlanta, Georgia 30333, is required for shipments of any etiological agent or insect, animal or plant vector of human disease or any exotic living insect, animal, or plant capable of being a vector of human disease.

18. Narcotic Drugs and Derivatives. The importation of controlled substances including narcotics, marijuana and other dangerous drugs is prohibited except when imported in compliance with regulations of the Drug Enforcement Administration of the Department of Justice, Washington, D.C. 20537. Examples of some of the prohibited controlled substances are amphetamines; barbiturates; coca leaves and derivatives such as cocaine; hallucinogenic substances such as LSD, mescaline, peyote, marijuana and other forms of cannabis; opiates including methadone; opium including opium derivatives, such as morphine and heroin; synthetic substitutes for narcotic drugs.

19. Drug Paraphernalia. Items of drug paraphernalia are prohibited from importation or exportation under Section 863, Title 21 of the United States Code. The term "drug paraphernalia" means any equipment, product, or material of any kind which is primarily intended or designed for use in manufacturing, compounding, converting, concealing, producing, processing, preparing, injecting, ingesting, inhaling, or otherwise introducing into the human body a controlled substance, possession of which is unlawful under the Controlled Substance Act (Title II of Public Law 91-513). Items of drug paraphernalia include, but are not limited to the following items:

a. Metal, wooden, acrylic, glass, stone, plastic, or ceramic pipes with or without screens, permanent screens, hashish heads, or punctured metal bowls;

b. water pipes;

c. carburetion tubes and devices;

d. smoking and carburetion masks;

e. roach clips: meaning objects used to hold burning material, such as a marijuana cigarette, that has become too small or too short to be held in the hand;

f. miniature spoons with level capacities of one-tenth cubic centimeter or less;

g. chamber pipes;

h. carburetor pipes;

i. electric pipes;

j. air-driven pipes;

k. chillums;

l. bongs;

m. ice pipes or chillers;

n. wired cigarette papers; or

o. cocaine freebase kits.

The penalty for violation of this section is imprisonment of not more than three years and fine under Title 18 of the United States Code.

Gold, Silver, Currency, Stamps

20. Gold and Silver. The provisions of the National Stamping Act, as amended (15 U.S.C. 291-300) are enforced by the Department of Justice, Washington, D.C. 20530. Articles made of gold or alloys thereof are prohibited importation into the United States if the gold content is one-half carat divergence below the indicated fineness. In the case of articles made of gold or gold alloys, including the solder and alloy of inferior fineness, a one-carat divergence below the indicated fineness is permitted. Articles marked "sterling" or "sterling silver" must assay at least 0.925 of pure silver with a 0.004 divergence allowed. Other articles of silver or silver alloys must assay not less than 0.004 part below the indicated fineness thereof. Articles marked "coin" or "coin silver" must contain at least 0.900 part pure silver with an allowable divergence therefrom of 0.004 part below.

A person placing articles of gold or silver bearing a fineness or quality mark such as 14K, sterling, etc., in the mail or in interstate commerce must place his name or registered trademark next to the fineness mark in letters the same size as the fineness mark. The trademark or name is not required at the time of importation; therefore, Customs has no direct responsibility for enforcement of the law. Persons making inquiry or seeking advice or interpretation of the law should consult the Department of Justice.

Articles bearing the words "United States Assay" are prohibited importations. Articles made wholly or in part of inferior metal and plated or filled with gold or silver or alloys thereof and which are marked with the degree of fineness must also be marked to indicate the plated or filled content, and in such cases, the use of the words "sterling" or "coin" is prohibited.

All restrictions on the purchase, holding, selling, or otherwise dealing with gold were removed effective December 31, 1974, and gold may be imported subject to the usual Customs entry requirements. Under the Hobby Protection Act, any imitation numismatic item must be plainly and permanently marked "copy"; those that do not comply are subject to seizure and forfeiture. Unofficial gold coin restrikes must be marked with the country of origin. It is advisable to obtain a copy of the legal proclamation under which the coins are issued or an affidavit of government sanction of coins should be secured from a responsible banking official if the proclamation is unavailable.

The importation of South African and Soviet gold coins is prohibited.

21. Counterfeit Articles. Articles bearing facsimiles or replicas of coins or securities of the United States or of any foreign country are prohibited importation. Counterfeits of coins in circulation in the United States; counterfeited, forged, or altered obligations or other securities of the United States or of any foreign government; plates, dies, or other apparatus which may be used in making any of the foregoing are prohibited importations.

22. Monetary Instruments. Under the Currency and Foreign Transactions Reporting Act, 31 USC 1101 et seq., if more than $10,000 in monetary instruments is transported or caused to be transported (including by mail or other means) on any occasion into or out of the United States, or if a person in the United States receives more than that amount, a report of the transaction, Customs Form 4790, must be filed with U.S. Customs. Monetary instruments include U.S. or foreign coin, currency, travelers checks, money orders, and negotiable instruments or investment securities in bearer form but do not include bank checks, travelers checks, or money orders made payable to the order of a named person which have not been endorsed or which bear restrictive endorsement.

23. Postage Stamps. Facsimiles of United States postage stamps are prohibited except those for philatelic, educational, historical, or newsworthy purposes. Further information should be obtained from the United States Secret Service, Department of the Treasury, Washington, D.C. 20223.

Pesticides, Toxic and Hazardous Substances

24. Pesticides. The importation into the United States of economic poisons and devices, including insecticides, Paris greens, lead arsenates, fungicides, herbicides, and rodenticides, is governed by the provisions of the Insecticide, Fungicide, and Rodenticide Act of 1947, as amended by the Federal Environment Pesticide Control Act of 1972. All imported pesticides are required to be registered in accordance with the criteria established by the Environmental Protection Agency (EPA), Office of Pesticides and Toxic Substances, Washington D.C. 20460. Devices, although not required to be registered, must not bear any statement, design, or graphic representation that is false or misleading in any particular. Importations of pesticides and devices will not be released from Customs custody unless a Notice of Arrival by the Office of Pesticides and Toxic Substances is presented to Customs.

25. Toxic Substances. The Toxic Substances Control Act, effective January 1, 1977, regulates the manufacturing, processing, distribution in commerce, use or disposal of any chemical substance or mixture that may present an unreasonable risk of injury to health and the environment. This includes importation of such substances into the United States. Importations will not be released from Customs custody unless proper certification of "compliance" or "exemption" from requirements of the Toxic Substances Control Act is presented to Customs. For further information from EPA, call (202) 260-7835.

26. Hazardous Substances. The importation into the United States of dangerous caustic or corrosive substances in packages suitable for household use and of hazardous substances is regulated by the Hazardous Substance Act; the Caustic Poison Act; the Food, Drug and Cosmetic Act; and the Consumer Product Safety Act. The marking, labeling, packaging, and transportation of hazardous materials, substances, wastes, and their containers is regulated by the Office of Hazardous Materials Transportation of the Department of Transportation, Washington, D.C. 20590.

Textile, Wool, and Fur Products

27. Textile Products. All textile fiber products imported into the United States shall be stamped, tagged, labeled, or otherwise marked with the following information as required by the Textile Fiber Products Identification Act, unless exempted from marking under section 12 of the Act:

a. The generic names and percentages by weight of the constituent fibers present in the textile fiber product, exclusive of permissive ornamentation, in amounts of more than 5 percent in order of predominance by weight, with any percentage of fiber or fibers required to be designated as "other fiber" or "other fibers" appearing last. Fibers present in amounts of 5 percent or less must be designated as "other fibers."

b. The name of the manufacturer or the name or registered identification number issued by the Federal Trade Commission of one or more persons marketing or handling the textile fiber product. A word trademark, used as a house mark, registered in the United States Patent Office, may be on labels in lieu of the name otherwise required if the owner of such trademark furnishes a copy of the registration to the Federal Trade Commission prior to use.

c. The name of the country where processed or manufactured.

For the purpose of the enforcement of the Textile Fiber Products Identification Act, a commercial invoice covering a shipment of textile fiber products exceeding $500 in value and subject to the labeling requirements of the Act is required to show the information noted in Chapter 6, in addition to that ordinarily required on the invoices.

Regulations and pamphlets containing the text of the Textile Fiber Products Identification Act may be obtained from the Federal Trade Commission, Washington, D.C. 20580.

28. Wool. Any product containing woolen fiber imported into the United States, with the exception of carpets, rugs, mats, upholsteries, and articles made more than 20 years prior to importation, shall be tagged, labeled, or otherwise clearly marked with the following information as required by the Wool Products Labeling Act of 1939:

a. The percentage of the total fiber weight of the wool product, exclusive of ornamentation not exceeding 5 percent of the total fiber weight of (1) wool, (2) recycled wool, (3) each fiber other than wool if the percent by weight of such fiber is 5 percent or more, and (4) the aggregate of all other fibers.

b. The maximum percent of the total weight of the wool product, of any nonfibrous loading, filling, or adulterating matter.

c. The name of the manufacturer or person introducing the product in commerce in the United States; i.e., the importer. If the importer has a registered identification number issued by the Federal Trade Commission, that number may be used instead of the individual's name.

For the purpose of the enforcement of the Wool Products Labeling Act, a commercial invoice covering a shipment of wool products exceeding $500 in value and subject to the labeling requirements of the act is required to show the information noted in Chapter 6.

The provisions of the Wool Products Labeling Act apply to products manufactured in the United States as well as to imported products.

Pamphlets containing the text of the Wool Products Labeling Act and the regulations may be obtained from the Federal Trade Commission, Washington, D.C. 20580.

29. Fur. Any article of wearing apparel made in whole or in part of fur or used fur, with the exception of articles that are made of new fur of which the cost or manufacturer's selling price does not exceed $7, imported into the United States shall be tagged, labeled, or otherwise clearly marked to show the following information as required by the Fur Products Labeling Act:

a. The name of the manufacturer or person introducing the product in commerce in the United States; i.e., the importer. If the importer has a registered identification number, that number may be used instead of the individual's name.

b. The name or names of the animal or animals that produced the fur as set forth in the Fur Products Name Guide and as permitted under the rules and regulations.

c. That the fur product contains used or damaged fur where such is the fact.

d. That the fur product is bleached, dyed, or otherwise artificially colored when such is the fact.

e. That the fur product is composed in whole or in substantial part of paws, tails, bellies, or waste fur when such is the fact.

f. The name of the country of origin of any imported furs contained in a fur product.

The entry or withdrawal from warehouse for consumption is prohibited for raw or not dressed, or dressed ermine, fox, kolinsky, marten, mink, muskrat, and weasel furs and skins which are products of the Union of Soviet Socialist Republics (Russia) which, at the time of entry or withdrawal from warehouse for consumption, is under Communist domination or control.

For the purpose of enforcement of the Fur Products Labeling Act, a commercial invoice covering a shipment exceeding $500 in value of furs or fur products is required to show the information noted in Chapter 6.

The provisions of the Fur Products Labeling Act apply to fur and fur products in the United States as well as to imported furs and fur products. Regulations and pamphlets containing the text of the Fur Products Labeling Act may be obtained from the Federal Trade Commission, Washington, D.C. 20580.

Trademarks, Trade Names, and Copyrights

30. Trademarks and Trade Names. Articles bearing counterfeit trademarks, or marks which copy or simulate a registered trademark of a United States or foreign corporation are prohibited importation, provided a copy of the U.S. trademark registration is filed with the Commissioner of Customs and recorded in the manner provided by regulations (19 CFR 133.1-133.7). The U.S. Customs Service also affords similar protection against unauthorized shipments bearing trade names which are recorded with Customs pursuant to regulations (19 CFR Part 133, Subpart B). It is also unlawful to import articles bearing genuine trademarks owned by a U.S. citizen or corporation without permission of the U.S. trademark owner, if the foreign and domestic trademark owners are not parent and subsidiary companies or otherwise under common ownership and control, provided the trademark has been recorded with Customs. (15 U.S.C. 1124; 19 U.S.C. 1526).

The Customs Reform and Simplification Act of 1978 strengthened the protection afforded trademark owners against the importation of articles bearing a counterfeit mark. A "counterfeit trademark" is defined as a spurious trademark which is identical with, or substantially indistinguishable from, a registered trademark. Articles bearing a counterfeit trademark which are seized by Customs and forfeited to the government may be (1) given to any Federal, state, or local government agency which has established a need for the article; (2) given to a charitable institution; or (3) sold at public auction if more than 1 year has passed since forfeiture and no eligible organization has established a need for the article. The counterfeit marks must be removed before the forfeited articles may be given away or sold. If this is not feasible, the articles are destroyed. The law also provides an exemption from all restrictions on trademarked articles (limited to one of each type) accompanying a person arriving in the United States when the articles are for personal use and not for sale.

31. Copyrights. Section 602(a) of the Copyright Revision Act of 1976 (17 U.S.C. 602(a)) provides that the importation into the United States of copies of a work acquired outside the United States without authorization of the copyright owner is an infringement of the copyright. Articles imported in violation of the import prohibitions are subject to seizure and forfeiture. Forfeited articles shall be destroyed; however, the articles may be returned to the country of export whenever Customs is satisfied that there was no intentional violation. The substantial similarity test is employed to determine if a design has been copied. Copyright owners seeking import protection from the U.S. Customs Service must register their claim to copyright with the U.S. Copyright Office and record their registration with Customs in accordance with applicable regulations (19 CFR Part 133, Subpart D).

Wildlife and Pets

32. Wildlife and Pets. The importation of live wild or game animals, birds, and other wildlife, or any part or product made therefrom, and the eggs of wild or game birds, is subject to certain prohibitions, restrictions, permit and quarantine requirements of several Government agencies. Importations of wildlife, parts, or their products must be entered at certain designated Customs ports of entry unless an exception is granted by the U.S. Fish and Wildlife Service, Department of the Interior, Washington, D.C. 20240.

On or after January 1, 1981, most firms (with some significant exceptions) importing or exporting wildlife must obtain a license from the Fish and Wildlife Service. Applications and further information may be obtained from the Fish and Wildlife Special Agent in Charge for the state in which the importer or exporter is located.

Endangered species of wildlife and certain species of animals and birds are generally prohibited entry into the United States and may be imported only under a permit granted by the U.S. Fish and Wildlife Service. Specific information concerning import requirements should be obtained from that agency.

Antique articles which would otherwise be prohibited under the Endangered Species Act may be admitted provided certain conditions are met. These articles must be entered at certain designated antique ports.

The taking and importation of marine mammals and their products are subject to the requirements of the Marine Mammal Protection Act of 1972 and cannot be imported without a permit from the National Marine Fisheries Service, National Oceanic and Atmospheric Administration, Washington, D.C. 20910, or the U.S. Fish and Wildlife Service.

Regulations to implement the Convention on International Trade in Endangered Species of Wild Fauna and Flora became effective on May 23, 1977. Certain animals, mammals, birds, reptiles, amphibians, fish, snails, and clams, may be prohibited or require permits or certification which may be obtained from the U.S. Fish and Wildlife Service.

The importation into the United States of any wild animal or bird is prohibited if the animal or bird was captured, taken, shipped, possessed, or exported contrary to the law of the foreign country or subdivision thereof. In addition, no wild animal or bird from any foreign country may be taken, purchased, sold or possessed contrary to the laws of any State, territory, or possession of the United States.

The importation of the feathers or skin of any wild bird, except for scientific and educational purposes, is prohibited. This prohibition does not apply to fully manufactured artificial flies used for fishing. The feathers of certain birds for use in the manufacture of artificial flies used for fishing or for millinery purposes may be imported under permit issued by the U.S. Fish and Wildlife Service.

Live birds protected under the Migratory Bird Treaty Act may be imported into the United States from foreign countries for scientific or propagating purposes only under permits issued by the U.S. Fish and Wildlife Service. These migratory birds and any game animals (e.g., antelope, mountain sheep, deer, bears, peccaries, squirrels, rabbits, and hares) imported from Mexico must be accompanied by Mexican export permits.

Importations in this class are also subject to the quarantine requirements of the Department of Agriculture and the United States Public Health Service. Appropriate inquiries in this respect should be directed to those agencies.

On June 9, 1989, the U.S. Fish and Wildlife Service announced a ban on the importation of all African elephant ivory and any products made from it. The ban covers all commercial and noncommercial shipments including household effects and personal baggage accompanying a tourist. For further information, contact the U.S. Fish and Wildlife Service, Washington, D.C. 20240.

The importation of birds, cats, dogs, monkeys, and turtles is subject to the requirements of the U.S. Public Health Service, Centers for Disease Control, Quarantine Division, Atlanta, Georgia 30333, and the Veterinary Services of the Animal and Plant Health Inspection Service, Department of Agriculture, Hyattsville, Maryland 20782.

The importation of turtles with a carapace length of less than four inches and psittacine birds are subject to the requirements of the Food and Drug Administration.

Other Miscellaneous Prohibited or Restricted Merchandise

White or yellow phosphorus matches, fireworks banned under Federal or State restrictions, pepper shells, switchblade knives, and lottery tickets are prohibited.

33. Foreign Assets Control Restrictions. The Office of Foreign Assets Control administers regulations (31 CFR, Chapter V) which generally prohibit the importation of merchandise or goods that contain components from the following countries: Cambodia, Cuba, Iran, Iraq, Libya, North Korea, and Vietnam.

These proscriptions do not apply to informational materials such as pamphlets, books, tapes, films, or recordings.

Specific licenses are required to bring prohibited merchandise into the United States, but they are rarely granted. Foreign visitors to the United States, however, may be permitted to bring in small articles for personal use as accompanied baggage, depending upon the goods' country of origin.

Travelers should be aware of certain travel restrictions that may apply to these countries. Because of the strict enforcement of these prohibitions, those anticipating foreign travel to any of the countries listed above would do well to write in advance to the Office of Foreign Assets Control, Department of the Treasury, Washington, D.C. 20220, or to call (202) 535-9445.

34. Obscene, Immoral, and Seditious Matter. Section 305, Tariff Act of 1930, as amended, prohibits the importation of any book, writing, advertisement, circular, or picture containing any matter advocating or urging treason or insurrection against the United States, or forcible resistance to any law of the United States, or containing any threat to take the life of or inflict bodily harm upon any person in the United States, or any obscene book, writing, advertisement, circular, picture or other representation figure, or image on or of paper or other material, or any instrument, or other article which is obscene or immoral, or any drug or medicine for causing unlawful abortion.

35. Petroleum and Petroleum Products. Importations of petroleum and petroleum products are subject to the requirements of the Department of Energy. An import license is no longer required. These importations may be subject to an oil import license fee collected and administered by the Department of Energy. Inquiries should be directed to the Department of Energy, Washington, D.C. 20585.

36. Products of Convict or Forced Labor. Merchandise produced, mined, or manufactured by means of the use of convict labor, forced labor, or indentured labor under penal sanctions is prohibited importation, provided a finding has been published pursuant to section 12.42 of the Customs Regulations (19 CFR 12.42), that certain classes of merchandise from a particular country, produced by convict, forced, or indentured labor, were either being, or are likely to be, imported into the United States in violation of section 307 of the Tariff Act of 1930, as amended (19 U.S.C. 1307).

37. Unfair Competition. Section 337 of the Tariff Act, as amended, prohibits the importation of merchandise if the President finds that unfair methods of competition or unfair acts exist. This section is most commonly invoked in the case of patent violations, although a patent need not be at issue. Prohibition of entries of the merchandise in question generally is for the term of the patent, although a different term may by specified.

Following a section 337 investigation, the International Trade Commission may find that unfair methods of competition or unfair acts exist with respect to the importation of certain merchandise. After the International Trade Commission has issued an order, the President is allowed 60 days to take action; should the 60 days expire without Presidential action, the order becomes final. During the 60-day period or until the President acts, importation of the merchandise is allowed under a special bond but it must be recalled by Customs if appropriate under the conditions of the order when it becomes final. If the President determines that entry of the merchandise is not in violation of section 337, the bond is canceled.

38. Steel and Machine Tools. Certain types of steel from various countries and certain machine tools from Japan and Taiwan are subject to Voluntary Restraint Arrangements (VRAs) negotiated by the United States Trade Representative and the individual countries. These are agreements by which the level of exports of the covered products are voluntarily limited by the exporting country. The VRAs are administered by the Department of Commerce and presentation of an export certificate or license by the country of origin is a condition of entry.

29 alcoholic beverages

Any person or firm wishing to engage in the business of importing distilled spirits, wines, or malt beverages into the United States must first obtain an importer's basic permit from the Bureau of Alcohol, Tobacco and Firearms, Department of the Treasury, Washington, D.C. 20226, Tel. (202) 927-8110. That agency is responsible for administering the Federal Alcohol Administration Act.

Distilled spirits imported in bulk containers of a capacity of more than one gallon may be withdrawn from Customs custody only by persons to whom it is lawful to sell or otherwise dispose of distilled spirits in bulk. Bulk or bottled shipments of imported spirits or distilled or intoxicating liquors must at the time of importation be accompanied by a copy of a bill of lading or other documents, such as an invoice, showing the name of the consignee, the nature of its contents, and the quantity contained therein (18 U.S.C. 1263).

U.S. Customs will not release alcoholic beverages destined to any State for use in violation of its laws, and the importation of alcoholic beverages in the mails is prohibited.

The United States adopted the metric system of measure with the enactment of the Metric Conversion Act of 1975. In general, imported wine must conform with the metric standards of fill if bottled or packed on or after January 1, 1979. Imported distilled spirits, with some exceptions, must conform with the metric standards of fill if bottled or packed on or after January 1, 1980. Distilled spirits and wines bottled or packed prior to the respective dates must be accompanied by a statement to that effect signed by a duly authorized official of the appropriate foreign country. This statement may be a separate document or be shown on the invoice. Malt beverages including beer are not subject to metric standards of fill.

Marking

If distilled spirits are bottled abroad in containers having a capacity of 200 milliliters or more, these containers must be legibly and permanently marked with (1) the words "Liquor Bottle" and (2) the city or country address of the manufacturer of the spirits or of the exporter abroad, or the city of address of the importer in the United States. Empty liquor bottles imported to be filled in the United States shall be marked with the words "Liquor Bottle" and the city or country of address of the bottle manufacturer. Empty or filled distinctive liquor bottles not bearing such indicia may be imported only with the approval of the Bureau of Alcohol, Tobacco and Firearms.

Imported wines in bottles and other containers are required to be packaged, marked, branded, and labeled in accordance with the regulations in 27 CFR Part 4. Imported malt beverages are also required to be labeled in conformance with the regulations in 27 CFR Part 7.

Each bottle, cask or other immediate container of imported distilled spirits, wines, or malt beverages must be marked for customs purposes to indicate the country of origin of the alcoholic beverage contained therein, unless the shipment comes within one of the exceptions outlined in Chapter 28 of this booklet.

Certificate of Label Approval

Labels affixed to bottles of imported distilled spirits and wine must be covered by certificates of label approval issued to the importer by the Bureau of Alcohol, Tobacco and Firearms. Certificates of label approval or photostatic copies must be filed with Customs before the goods may be released for sale in the United States. Certificate of label approval requirements must also be met for fermented malt beverages if similar to the Federal requirements (27 CFR Parts 4, 5 and 7).

Foreign Documentation

Importers of wines and distilled spirits should consult the Bureau of Alcohol, Tobacco and Firearms about foreign documentation required; for example, certificates or origin, age, etc.

Requirements of Other Agencies

In addition, importation of alcoholic beverages is subject to the specific requirements of the Food and Drug Administration. Certain plant materials when used for bottle jackets for wine or other liquids are subject to special restrictions under plant quarantine regulations of the Animal and Plant Health Inspection Service. All bottle jackets made of dried or unmanufactured plant materials are subject to inspection upon arrival and are referred to the Department of Agriculture.

Wines or other distilled spirits from 13 countries require original certificates of origin as a condition of entry: Bulgaria, Canada, Chile, France, Federal Republic of Germany, Republic of Ireland, Jamaica, Mexico, Portugal, Romania, Spain, United Kingdom, and the USSR.

Public Law 100-690, codified under section 213-219A, requires that a health warning appear on the labels of containers of alcoholic beverages bottled on or after Nov. 18, 1989:

Government Warning: (1) According to the Surgeon General, women should not drink alcoholic beverages during pregnancy because of the risks of birth defects. (2) Consumption of alcoholic beverages impairs your ability to drive a car or operate machinery and may cause health problems.

Automobiles, Vehicles and Vehicle Equipment

Safety and Bumper Standards. As a general rule, all imported motor vehicles and items of motor vehicle equipment must comply with all applicable Federal Motor Vehicle Safety Standards in effect when these vehicles or items were manufactured. A Customs inspection at the time of entry will determine such compliance, which is verified by the original manufacturer's certification affixed to the vehicle or merchandise. A declaration, HS form 7, must be filed when motor vehicles or items of motor vehicle equipment are entered. HS form 7 can be obtained from customs brokers or ports of entry.

Certain temporary importations are exempt from the requirements for certification and conformance, including vehicles brought in for test and experimentation, training or demonstration, or brought in for use by nonresidents or members of foreign delegations or armed forces. Motor vehicles and motor vehicle equipment imported solely with the intention of exportation and so labeled are also exempt from these requirements.

A DOT bond in the amount of 150 percent of the dutiable value must be posted at the port of entry when a noncertified or nonconforming vehicle is imported for permanent use. This bond is intended to assure conformance of the vehicle within 120 days after entry. Unless specifically excepted, the importer must also sign a contract with a DOT-registered importer who will modify the vehicle to conform with all applicable safety and bumper standards, and who can certify the modification(s). A copy of this contract must be furnished to the Customs Service at the port of entry. Furthermore, the vehicle model and model year must, prior to entry, be determined to be eligible for importation. Federal regulations 49 CFR, parts 593 and 594 specify the petitioning process and fees required to obtain such a determination of eligibility.

An individual who has been employed outside the United States continuously since October 31,1988, who wishes to import a nonconforming vehicle acquired on or before October 31,1988, and who has not previously imported a nonconforming vehicle, may, until October 31,1992, import the vehicle directly. This vehicle must be brought into conformance within 120 days of entry, and the importer must submit a statement of compliance identifying the person or company that brought the vehicle into compliance and that describes the exact nature and extent of the modifications performed.

For additional information or details on these requirements, contact the U.S. Department of Transportation, National Highway Traffic Safety Administration, Director of the Office of Vehicle Safety Compliance (NEF-32), 400 Seventh Street, S.W., Washington, D.C. 20590.

A Final Word of Caution: The modifications required to bring nonconforming vehicles into compliance may be so extensive and costly that it may be impractical and even impossible to achieve such compliance. Moreover, under Federal Regulations 49 CFR parts 591 through 594, effective January 31,1990, some vehicle models are prohibited from importation altogether. It is highly recommended that these prohibitions and modifications be investigated before a vehicle is purchased for importation.

Emission Standards. The Clean Air Act, as amended, prohibits the importation into the United States of any motor vehicle or motor vehicle engine not in conformity with emission standards prescribed by the U.S. Environmental Protection Agency. For imported vehicles, these standards apply whether the vehicle is new or used. Vehicles imported for display, repair, alteration, racing, or testing are allowed entry provided they are not sold and approval is obtained from EPA prior to importation.

In addition to passenger cars, certain trucks, multipurpose vehicles (e.g. campers), motorcycles, etc., are subject to EPA standards. All complying 1971 and later models are required to have a label in a readily visible position in the engine compartment stating that the vehicle conforms to U.S. standards. This label will read "Vehicle Emission Control Information" and include the full corporate name, trademark of the manufacturer, and a statement that the vehicle meets U.S. EPA emission requirements. If this label is not present, the importer should verify conformity with the manufacturer.

A declaration, EPA Form 3520-1 (Rev. 3-91), is required to be filed at the time of entry for all nonconforming importations. Generally, a nonconforming vehicle or engine imported on or after July 1, 1988, must be imported through a currently qualified EPA-certified Independent Commercial Importer (ICI), unless approval is obtained from EPA prior to importation.

For further information including details of anticipated requirements and procedures, contact: Environmental Protection Agency, Investigation/Imports Section (EN-340F), Wash., D.C. 20460. Tel. (202) 260-2504.

Word of Caution. Modifications necessary to bring a nonconforming vehicle into conformity with the safety and bumper standards and/or emission standards may require extensive engineering, be impractical or impossible, or the labor and materials may be unduly expensive. Moreover, on or after July 1, 1988, it may not be possible to import certain models. These models must be exported or destroyed.

Boat Safety Standards

Imported boats and associated equipment are subject to U.S. Coast Guard safety regulations or standards under the Federal Boat Safety Act of 1971. Products subject to standards must have a compliance certification label affixed. Certain hulls also require a hull identification number to be affixed. A U.S. Coast Guard import declaration is required to be filed with entries of nonconforming boats. Further information may be obtained from the Commandant, U.S. Coast Guard, Washington, D.C. 20593.

Dutiability

Vessels that are brought into the United States for use in trade or commerce are not dutiable. Yachts or pleasure boats brought into the United States by nonresidents for their own use in pleasure cruising are also not dutiable. Yachts or pleasure boats owned by a resident or brought into the United States for sale or charter to a resident are dutiable. Further information may be found in U.S. Customs pamphlet "Pleasure Boats."

Restrictions on Use

Vessels that are foreign-built or of foreign registry may be used in the United States for pleasure purposes and in the foreign trade of the United States. However, Federal law prohibits the use of such vessels in the coastwise trade, i.e. the transportation of passengers or merchandise between points in the United States, including carrying fishing parties for hire. Questions concerning the use of foreign-built or foreign-flag vessels should be addressed to Chief, Carrier Rulings Branch, U.S. Customs Service, 1301 Constitution Ave., N.W., Washington, D.C. 20229.

31 import quotas

An import quota is a quantity control on imported merchandise for a certain period of time. Quotas are established by legislation, by directives and by proclamations issued under the authority contained in specific legislation. The majority of import quotas are administered by the U.S. Customs Service. The Commissioner of Customs controls the importation of quota merchandise but has no authority to change or modify any quota. United States import quotas may be divided into two types: *absolute* and *tariff-rate*.

Tariff-rate quotas provide for the entry of a specified quantity of the quota product at a reduced rate of duty during a given period. There is no limitation on the amount of the product which may be entered during the quota period, but quantities entered in excess of the quota for the period are subject to higher duty rates. In most cases, products of Communist-controlled areas are not entitled to the benefits of tariff-rate quotas.

Absolute quotas are quantitative; that is, no more than the amount specified may be permitted entry during a quota period. Some absolute quotas are global, while others are allocated to specified foreign countries. Imports in excess of a specified quota may be exported or warehoused for entry in a subsequent quota period.

The usual customs procedures generally applicable to other imports apply with respect to commodities subject to quota limitations.

The quota status of a commodity subject to a tariff-rate quota cannot be determined in advance of its entry. The quota rates of duty are ordinarily assessed on such commodities entered from the beginning of the quota period until such time in the period as it is determined that imports are nearing the quota level. District directors of Customs are then instructed to require the deposit of estimated duties at the over-quota duty rate and to report the time of official presentation of each entry. A final determination of the date and time when a quota is filled is made, and all district directors are advised accordingly.

Some of the absolute quotas are invariably filled at or shortly after the opening of the quota period. Each of these quotas is therefore officially opened at 12 noon E.S.T. on the designated effective date. When the total quantity for which entries filed at the opening of the quota period exceeds the quota, the merchandise is released on a pro rata basis, the pro rata being the ratio between the quota quantity and the total quantity offered for entry. This assures an equitable distribution of the quota.

Merchandise is not regarded as presented for purposes of determining quota priority until an entry summary or withdrawal from warehouse for consumption has been submitted in proper form and the merchandise is located within the port limits.

Commodities Subject to Quotas Administered by Customs

As provided in the Harmonized Tariff Schedule of the United States, the commodities listed below are subject to quota limitations in effect as of the date of publication of this booklet. Local Customs officers can be consulted about any changes. Information may also be obtained by contacting the Quota Branch, U.S. Customs Service, 1301 Constitution Avenue NW, Washington, D.C. 20229. (202) 566-8592.

Tariff-Rate Quotas

Milk and cream, not concentrated nor containing added sugar or other sweetening matter, of a fat content–by weight–exceeding one percent but not six percent.

Anchovies, in oil, in airtight containers.

Mandarins (Satsumas) in airtight containers.

Certain olives.

Tuna Fish

Whiskbrooms wholly or in part of broom corn.

Other brooms wholly or in part of broom corn.

Certain textiles assembled in Guam.

Certain sugars, syrups and molasses derived from sugarcane or sugar beets, except those entered pursuant to a license issued by the Secretary of Agriculture.

Certain textiles from Canada.

Absolute Quotas

Certain ethyl alcohol.

Certain tungstic acid and ammonium paratungstate.

Milk and cream, condensed or evaporated.

Butter substitutes, containing over 45 percent of butterfat.

Animal feeds containing milk or milk derivatives.

Buttermix containing over 5.5 percent but not over 45 percent by weight of butterfat.

Chocolate, containing 5.5 percent or less by weight of butterfat.

Chocolate crumb and other related articles containing over 5.5 percent by weight of butterfat.

Ice cream.

Peanuts, shelled or not shelled, blanched or otherwise prepared or preserved (except peanut butter).

Certain Cheddar cheese.

Cotton, not carded, not combed and not otherwise processed:

Having a staple length under 28.575 mm; and

Having a staple length 28.575 mm or more but under 34.925 mm; and

Having a staple length 34.925 mm or more.

Card strips made from cotton having a staple length under 30.1625 mm, and cotton comber waste, lap waste, sliver waste and roving waste.

Fibers of cotton processed but not spun.

Upland cotton.

Certain sugar blends.

Fluid milk and sweet or sour cream of a fat content by weight exceeding six percent but not 45 percent.

Textile articles and wearing apparel from certain countries.

Textile Articles

The U.S. Customs Service administers import controls of certain cotton, wool, man-made fiber articles, silk blends and other vegetable fibers manufactured or produced in designated countries. These controls are imposed on the basis of directives issued to the Commissioner of Customs by the Chairman of the Committee for the Implementation of Textile Agreements.

Information concerning specific import controls in effect and visa requirements may be obtained from the Commissioner of Customs. Other information concerning the textile program may be obtained from the Chairman, Committee for the Implementation of Textile Agreements, U.S. Department of Commerce, Washington, D.C. 20230.

Quotas or Licenses Administered by Other Government Agencies

Watches and Watch Movements. The Departments of Interior and Commerce administer the import quotas on watches and watch movements from insular possessions admissible free of duty under the statistical notes (91/5) to Chapter 91 of the Harmonized Tariff Schedules, on a licensing basis. Information concerning licenses may be obtained from Statutory Import Programs Staff, Import Administration, International Trade Administration, U.S. Department of Commerce, Washington, D.C. 20230.

Dairy Products. Certain dairy products listed below are subject to annual import quotas assigned by the Department of Agriculture and may be imported only under import licenses issued by that department. These quotas are administered through the U.S. Customs Service. Detailed information on the licensing of these products, or the conditions under which limited quantities may be imported without licenses, may be obtained from the Import Licensing Group, Foreign Agricultural Service, Room 5531-S, U.S. Department of Agriculture, Washington, D.C. 20250, Tel. (202) 447-2916.

Butter.

Dried cream.

Malted milk and compounds or mixtures of or substitutes for milk or cream.

Dried whole milk.

Dried skimmed milk.

Dried buttermilk and whey.

Cheddar cheese, and cheese and substitutes for cheese containing or processed from Cheddar cheese curd, and granular cheese and cheese substitutes for cheese containing or processed from such American-type cheese.

Cheese and substitutes for cheese containing, or processed from Edam and Gouda cheese.

Swiss or Emmenthaler cheese with eye formation; Gruyere-process cheese, and cheese and substitutes for cheese containing, or processed from, such cheese.

Edam and Gouda cheese.

Blue mold (except Stilton) cheese, and cheese and substitutes for cheese containing, or processed from, blue-mold cheese.

Italian-type cheeses, made from cow's milk, in original loaves (Romano made from cow's milk, Reggiano, Parmesano, Provoloni, Provolette, and Sbrinz).

Italian-type cheese, not in original loaves.

American-type cheese, including Colby, washed curd and granular cheese and cheese substitutes for cheese containing, or processed from such American-type cheese.

Cheese and substitutes for cheese (except *** cheese *** containing no butterfat or not over 0.5 percent by weight of butterfat***).

Cheese and substitutes for cheese, containing 0.5 percent or less by weight of butterfat.

Section 592 of the Tariff Act of 1930, as amended (19 U.S.C. 1592), generally provides that any person who by fraud, gross negligence, or negligence, enters, introduces, or attempts to introduce merchandise into the commerce of the United States by means of any material and false written or oral statement, document or act, or by any omission which is material, will be subject to a monetary penalty. The person's merchandise may be seized, in certain circumstances, to insure payment of the penalty and forfeited if the penalty is not paid.

This civil fraud statute has been applied by the Customs Service in cases involving individuals and companies in the United States and abroad which have negligently or intentionally provided false information concerning importations into the United States.

A criminal fraud statute also provides for sanctions to those presenting false information to Customs officers. Title 18, United States Code, section 542, provides a maximum of 2 years' imprisonment, a $5,000 fine, or both, for each violation involving an importation or attempted importation. Additionally, the Money Laundering Control Act of 1986 and the Anti-Drug Abuse Act of 1988, created and amended Federal laws relating to criminal activities commonly known as "money laundering." The Acts created 11 criminal and one civil offense that enable the government to seize and forfeit property involved in or traceable to property involved in Money Laundering or Bank Secrecy Act violations. Importation fraud violations are included as specified unlawful activities or predicate offenses within the Act. Penalties include imprisonment for up to 20 years for each offense and fines of up to $500,000.

Both of these statutes were enacted by Congress to discourage persons from evading the payment of lawful duties owed to the United States, although these laws apply today, whether or not the United States is deprived of lawful duties. They are enforced by special agents assigned to the Office of Enforcement who operate throughout the United States and in major trading centers of the world. Suspected or known violations of any law involved with the importation of merchandise into the United States can be reported toll free and anonymously by calling 1-800 BE-ALERT (232-5378). Rewards are applicable in many instances associated with the reporting of fraud.

33   foreign-trade zones

Foreign or "free" trade zones are secured areas legally outside a nation's customs territory. Their purpose is to attract and promote international trade and commerce. The Foreign-Trade Zones Board authorizes operations based upon showing that the intended operations are not detrimental to the public interest. Subzones are special-purpose facilities for companies unable to operate effectively at public zone sites. Foreign-trade zones are usually located in or near Customs ports of entry, at industrial parks, or terminal warehouse facilities. Foreign-trade zones must be within 60 miles or 90 minutes' driving time from the Customs supervising office, while subzones have no limit and are located in the zone user's private facility. A Foreign-Trade Zones Board, created by the Foreign-Trade Zones Act of 1934, reviews and approves applications to establish, operate, and maintain foreign-trade zones. It is important to note that although foreign-trade zones are legally outside the Customs territory of the United States, other federal laws, such as the Federal Food, Drug, and Cosmetic Act, are applicable to products and establishments with such zones.

Foreign exporters planning to expand or open up new American outlets may forward their goods to a foreign-trade zone in the United States to be held for an unlimited period while awaiting a favorable market in the United States or nearby countries without being subject to customs entry, payment of duty or tax, or bond.

Treatment of Goods

Merchandise lawfully brought into these wines may be stored, sold, exhibited, broken up, repacked, assembled, distributed, sorted, graded, cleaned, mixed with foreign or domestic merchandise, or otherwise manipulated or manufactured. However, imported merchandise for use in the zone, such as construction material and production equipment, must be entered for consumption before it is taken into a zone. The Foreign-Trade Zones Board may determine, however, that an operation is not in the public interest. The resulting merchandise may thereafter be either exported or transferred into customs territory. When foreign goods, in their condition at time of entry into the zone or after processing there, are transferred into customs territory of the United States, the goods must be entered at the customhouse. If entered for consumption, duties and taxes will be assessed on the entered articles, according to the condition of the foreign merchandise at the time of entry into the zone, if it has been placed in the status of privileged foreign merchandise prior to manipulation or manufacture, or on the basis of its condition at the time of entry for consumption, if the foreign merchandise was placed under nonprivileged status at the time of entry into the zone. Merchandise may be considered exported, for Customs or other purposes, upon its admission to a zone in zone-restricted status; however, the merchandise taken into a zone under zone-restricted status may be for the sole purpose of exportation, destruction (except destruction of distilled spirits, wines, and fermented malt liquors) or storage.

An important feature of foreign-trade zones for foreign merchants entering the American market is that the goods may be brought to the threshold of the market, making immediate delivery certain and avoiding possible cancellation of orders due to shipping delays after a favorable market has closed.

Production of articles in zones by the combined use of domestic and foreign materials makes unnecessary either the sending of the domestic materials abroad for manufacture or the duty-paid or bonded importation of the foreign materials. Duties on the foreign goods involved in such processing or manufacture are payable only on the actual quantity of such foreign goods incorporated in merchandise transferred from a zone for entry into the commerce of the United States. If there is any unrecoverable waste resulting from manufacture or manipulation, allowances are made for it, thereby eliminating payment of duty except on the articles which are actually entered. If there is any recoverable waste, it is dutiable only in its condition as such and in the quantity entered.

Another feature under the zone act is the authority to exhibit merchandise within a zone. Zone facilities may be utilized for the full exhibition of foreign merchandise without bond, for an unlimited length of time, and with no requirement of exportation or duty payment. Thus, the owner of goods in a zone may display his goods where they are stored, establish showrooms of his own, or join with other importers in displaying his merchandise in a permanent exhibition established in the zone; and, since he may also store and process merchandise in a zone, he is not limited to mere display of samples, but he may sell from stock in wholesale quantities. Retail trade is prohibited in zones.

The owner of foreign merchandise that has not been manipulated or manufactured in any way that would effect a change in its United States tariff classification had it been taken into customs territory when first imported may, upon request to the district director of Customs, have its dutiable status fixed and liquidated. This dutiable status will apply irrespective of when the merchandise is entered into customs territory and even though its condition or form may have been changed by processing in the zone, as indicated above.

Domestic merchandise may be taken into a zone and, providing its identity is maintained in accordance with regulations, may be returned to customs territory free of quotas, duty, or tax, even though while in the zone it may have been combined with or made part of other articles. However, domestic distilled spirits, wine, and beer, and a limited number of other kinds of merchandise generally may not be processed while in the zone.

Advantages

Savings may result from manipulations and manufacture in a zone. For example, many products, shipped to the zone in bulk, can be dried, sorted, graded, or cleaned and bagged or packed, permitting savings of duties and taxes on moisture taken from content or on dirt removed and culls thrown out. From incoming shipments of packaged or bottled goods, damaged packages or broken bottles can be removed. Where evaporation results during shipment or while goods are stored in the zone, contents of barrels or other containers can be regauged and savings obtained, as no duties are payable on the portions lost or removed. In other words, barrels or other containers can be gauged at the time of transfer to customs territory to insure that duties will not be charged on any portion of their contents which has been lost due to evaporation, leakage, breakage, or otherwise. These operations may also be conducted in bonded warehouses.

Savings in shipping charges, duties, and taxes may result from such operations as shipping unassembled or disassembled furniture, machinery, etc., to the zone and assembling or reassembling it there.

Merchandise may be remarked or relabeled in the zone (or in a bonded warehouse) to conform to requirements for entry into the commerce of the United States if otherwise up to standard. Remarking or relabeling that would be misleading is not permitted in the zone. Substandard foods and drugs may, in certain cases, be reconditioned to meet the requirements of the Food, Drug, and Cosmetics Act.

There is no time limit as to how long foreign merchandise may be stored in a zone, or when it must be entered into customs territory, reexported, or destroyed.

Transfer of Goods in Bonded Warehouses

Foreign merchandise in Customs bonded warehouses may be transferred to the zone at any time before the limitation on its retention in the bonded warehouse expires, but such a transfer to the zone may be made only for the purpose of eventual exportation, destruction, or permanent storage.

When foreign merchandise is transferred to the zone from Customs bonded warehouses, the bond is cancelled and all obligations in regard to duty payment, or as to the time when the merchandise is to be reexported, are terminated. Similarly, the owner of domestic merchandise stored in Internal Revenue bonded warehouses may transfer his goods to a zone and obtain cancellation of bonds. In addition, domestic goods moved into a zone under zone restricted status are considered exported upon entering the zone for purposes of excise and other internal revenue tax rebates. A manufacturer, operating in customs territory and using dutiable imported materials in his product, may also obtain drawback of duties paid or cancellation of bond, upon transferring the product to the zone for export and complying with the appropriate regulations.

Location of, and general information on United States Foreign-Trade Zones may be obtained from the Foreign-Trade Zones Board, Department of Commerce, Washington, D.C. 20230. Questions relating to legal aspects of Customs Service responsibilities in regard to foreign trade zones should be addressed to: Chief, Entry Rulings Branch, U.S. Customs Service, 1301 Constitution Avenue, N.W., Washington, D.C. 20229. Questions relating to operational aspects of such responsibilities should be addressed to the appropriate district/area director of Customs. The Foreign-Trade Zones Manual for grantees, operators, users, Customshouse brokers, may be purchased from the Superintendent of Documents, U.S. Government Printing Office, Washington, D.C. 20402. When ordering refer to GPO Stock No. 048-002-00111-7 and Customs Publication No. 559. The cost is $13.00; $16.20 for foreign mailing.

appendix

1 Invoices

Type of Invoice Required—Section 141.83, Customs Regulations 65

Pro Forma Invoice 66

Special Summary Steel Invoice, Form 5520 67

2 Additional Information Required for Certain Classes of Merchandise—Section 141.89, Customs Regulations 68

3 Customs Valuation—Tariff Act of 1930. Sec. 402 19 U.S.C. 1401a 74

4 Other Forms

Carrier's Certificate 82

CF 5291—Power of Attorney 82

CF 5297—Corporate Surety Power of Attorney 83

CF 301—Customs Bond 84–85

CF 7501—Entry Summary 86

1 invoices

§ 141.83 Type of invoice required.

(a) *Special Customs Invoice.*

The requirement for a special Customs invoice was eliminated by the Customs Service effective May 10, 1985. Importers bringing commercial shipments with transaction value of $500 or more into the United States will provide a commercial invoice containing the data required by Section 141.86 of the Customs Regulations. The commercial invoice should also show the country of origin of the merchandise, all goods or services furnished for the production of the merchandise (e.g. assists such as dies, molds, tools, engineering work) not included in the invoice price, and each invoice should identify by name a responsible individual who has knowledge of the facts of the transaction.

(b) *Special summary invoice.*

A special summary invoice shall be presented for each shipment of merchandise described in § 141.89(b). The district director may waive production of a special Customs invoice (Customs Form 5515) if a special summary invoice is required. [TD 78–53.]

(c) *Commercial invoice.*

(1) A commercial invoice shall be filed for each shipment of imported merchandise not required by paragraph (a) to have a special Customs invoice and not exempted by paragraph (d) from both a special Customs invoice and a commercial invoice. The commercial invoice shall be prepared in the manner customary in trade, contain the information required by Sections 141.86 through 141.89, and substantiate the statistical information required by Section 141.61(e) to be given on the entry, entry summary, or withdrawal documentation.

(2) The district director may accept a copy of a required commercial invoice in place of the original. A copy, other than a photostatic or photography copy, shall contain a declaration by the foreign seller, the shipper, or the importer that it is a true copy. [TDs 78–53, 79–221.]

(d) *Special Customs or commercial invoice not required.*

A special Customs invoice or a commercial invoice shall not be required in connection with the filing of the entry, entry summary, or withdrawal documentation for merchandise listed in this paragraph. The importer, however, shall present any invoice, memorandum invoice or bill pertaining to the merchandise which may be in his possession or available to him. If no invoice or bill is available, a pro forma (or substitute) invoice, as provided for in Section 141.85, shall be filed, and shall contain information adequate for the examination of merchandise and the determination of duties, and information and documentation which verify the information required for statistical purposes by Section 141.61 (e) to be given on the entry, entry summary, or withdrawal documentation.

(1) Merchandise having an aggregate purchase price or value, as specified in paragraph (a) of this section, of $500 or less.

(2) Merchandise not intended for sale or any commercial use in its imported condition or any other form, and not brought in on commission for any person other than the importer.

(3) [Reserved.]

(4) [Reserved.]

(5) Merchandise returned to the United States after having been exported for repairs or alteration under item 9802.00.04 or 9802.00.60, Harmonized Tariff Schedule of the United States (19 U.S.C. 1202).

(6) Merchandise shipped abroad, not delivered to the consignee, and returned to the United States.

(7) Merchandise exported from continuous Customs custody within 6 months after the date of entry.

(8) Merchandise consigned to, or entered in the name of, any agency of the U.S. Government.

(9) Merchandise for which an appraisement entry is accepted.

(10) Merchandise entered under a temporary importation bond or a permanent exhibition bond.

(11) Merchandise provided for in section 465 or 466, Tariff Act of 1930 (19 U.S.C. 1465 or 1466), which pertain to certain equipment, repair parts, and supplies for vessels.

(12) Merchandise imported as supplies, stores, and ｊuipment of the importing carrier and subsequently made subject to entry pursuant to section 466, Tariff Act of 1930, as amended (19 U.S.C. 1446).

(13) Ballast (not including cargo used for ballast) landed from a vessel and delivered for consumption.

(14) Merchandise, whether privileged or nonprivileged, resulting from manipulation or manufacture in a foreign trade zone.

(15) Screenings contained in bulk importations of grain or seeds.

Note: *The requirement for a special Customs invoice was waived by the Customs Service on March 1, 1982. However, it may still be used. If a commercial invoice is used, it must be signed by the seller and shipper or their agents.*

PRO FORMA INVOICE

Importers Statement of Value or the Price Paid in the Form of an Invoice

Not being in possession of a special or commercial seller's or shipper's invoice I request that you accept the statement of value or the price paid in the form of an invoice submitted below:

Name of shipper _____ address _____

Name of seller _____ address _____

Name of consignee _____ address _____

Name of purchaser _____ address _____

The merchandise (has) (has not) been purchased or agreed to be purchased by me. The prices, or in the case of consigned goods the values, given below are true and correct to the best of my knowledge and belief, and are based upon (check basis with an "X"):

(a) The prices paid or agreed to be paid ( ) as per order dated _____

(b) Advices from exporters by letter ( ) by cable ( ) dated _____

(c) Comparative values of shipments previously received ( ) dated _____

(d) Knowledge of the market in the country of exportation ( )

(e) Knowledge of the market in the United States (if U.S. value) ( )

(f) Advices of the District Director of Customs ( )

(g) Other ( )

A	B	C	D	E	F	G
Case marks numbers	Manufacturer's item number symbol or brand	Quantities and full description	Unit purchase price (currency)	Total purchase price (currency)	Unit foreign value	Total foreign value

Check which of the charges below are, and which are not, included in the prices listed in columns "D" and "E":

Amount Included   Not Included

Amount Included   Not Included

Packing_____

Cartage_____

Inland freight_____

Wharfage and loading
   abroad_____

Country of origin_____

Lighterage_____

Ocean freight_____

U.S. duties_____

Other charges (identify by
   name and amount_____

Total_____

If any other invoice is received, I will immediately file it with the District Director of Customs.

Date _____   Signature of person making invoice _____

Title and firm name _____

DEPARTMENT OF THE TREASURY
UNITED STATES CUSTOMS SERVICE
19 U.S.C. 1481, 1482, 1484

SPECIAL SUMMARY STEEL INVOICE
19 CFR 141.89(b)
(Prepare in Duplicate)

FORM APPROVED.
O.M.B. No. 1515-0083

4. CODES FOR COLUMN 18
- C - Width
- D - Length
- E - Edging
- F - Chemistry
- G - Quality (e.g. commercial deep drawing)
- H - Heat treating
- I - Coating
- J - Inspection and testing
- K - Surface treatments
- OTHER(S)--Specify:
- L -
- M -
- N -

1. SELLER	**2. DOCUMENT NO.**
	3. INVOICE NO. AND DATE
6. PRODUCER IF OTHER THAN SELLER (Name and Address)	**5. REFERENCES**
	7. BUYER
8. IMPORTER	Importer of Record? ☐ Yes ☐ No
	9. ORIGIN OF GOODS
	10. DATE PRICE TERMS AGREED / **11. CURRENCY/EXCH RATE** (If fixed or Agreed)
	12. TERMS OF SALE, PAYMENTS AND DISCOUNTS

13. MARKS AND NUMBERS	14. AISI Category	15. DESCRIPTION OF GOODS (INCLUDE SPECIFICATIONS)	16. QUANTITY	17. BASE PRICE	18. EXTRAS a. code	18. EXTRAS b. price	19. UNIT PRICE a. home mkt	19. UNIT PRICE b. invoice	19. UNIT PRICE c. resale	20. INVOICE TOTALS

21. ☐ If the production of these goods involved furnishing goods or services to the seller (*e.g., assists such as dies, molds, tools, engineering work*) and the value is not included in the invoice price, check Box 21 and explain above.

23. PACKING COSTS	
24. TRANSPORTATION COSTS TO POINT OF EXPORTATION	
25. OCEAN, AIR, OR INTERNATIONAL FREIGHT	
26. INSURANCE COSTS	
27. FREIGHT FROM U.S. POINT OF IMPORTATION	
28. OTHER COSTS *(Specify)*	

22. DECLARATION OF SELLER/SHIPPER (OR AGENT)
I declare:

(A) ☐ If there are any commissions, rebates, drawbacks, or bounties allowed upon exportation of goods, I have checked Box (A) and itemized separately above.

(B) ☐ If any unrelated incentives or reimbursements of dumping duties, or other inducements not reflected in this invoice have been, or will be, paid, granted, or received in connection with the sale of these goods, I have checked Box (B) and explained above.

I further declare that there is no other invoice differing from this one (unless otherwise described above) and that all statements contained in this invoice and declaration are true and correct.

SIGNATURE OF SELLER/SHIPPER (OR AGENT): **X**

31. DECLARATION OF IMPORTER (When providing information)

Merchandise ☐ has ☐ has not been resold as of this date.

IMPORTER SIGNATURE: **X**

DATE:

29. DUTY
30. SELLING EXPENSES & PROCESSING

Customs Form 5520 (090685)

67

2 additional information

§ 141.89 Additional Information for certain classes of merchandise.

(A) Invoices for the following classes of merchandise, classifiable under the Harmonized Tariff Schedule of the United States (HTSUS), shall set forth the additional information specified: [75–42, 75–239, 78–53, 83–251, 84–149.]

Aluminum and alloys of aluminum classifiable under subheadings 7601.10.60, 7601.20.60, 7601.20.90, or 7602.00.00, HTSUS (T.D. 53092, 55977, 56143)—Statement of the percentages by weight of any metallic element contained in the article.

Articles manufactured of textile materials, Coated or laminated with plastics or rubber, classifiable in Chapter(s) 39, 40, and 42—Include a description indicating whether the fabric is coated or laminated on both sides, on the exterior surface or on the interior surface.

Bags manufactured of plastic sheeting and not of a reinforced or laminated construction, classified in Chapter 39 or in heading 4202—Indicate the gauge of the plastic sheeting.

Ball or roller bearings classifiable under subheading 8482.10.50 through 8482.80.00, HTSUS (T.D. 68–306)—(1) Type of bearing (i.e. whether a ball or roller bearing); (2) If a roller bearing, whether a spherical, tapered, cylindrical, needled or other type; (3) Whether a combination bearing (i.e. a bearing containing both ball and roller bearings, etc.); and (4) If a ball bearing (not including ball bearing with integral shafts or parts of ball bearings), whether or not radial, the following: (a) outside diameter of each bearing; and (b) whether or not a radial bearing (the definition of radial bearing is, for Customs purposes, an antifriction bearing primarily designed to support a load perpendicular to shaft axis).

Beads (T.D. 50088, 55977)—(1) The length of the string, if strung; (2) The size of the beads expressed in millimeters; (3) The material of which the beads are composed, i.e. ivory, glass, imitation pearl, etc.

Bed Linen and Bedspreads—Statement as to whether or not the article contains any embroidery, lace, braid, edging, trimming, piping or applique work.

Chemicals—Furnish the use and Chemical Abstracts Service number of chemical compounds classified in Chapters 27, 28 and 29, HTSUS.

Colors, dyes, stains and related products provided for under heading 3204, HTSUS—The following information is required: (1) Invoice name of product; (2) Trade name of product; (3) Identity and percent by weight of each component; (4) Color Index number (if none, so state); (5) Color Index generic name (if none so state); (6) Chemical Abstracts Service number of the active ingredient; (7) Class of merchandise (state whether acid type dye, basic dye, disperse dye, fluorescent brightener, soluble dye, vat dye, toner or other (describe); (8) Material to which applied (name the material for which the color, dye, or toner is primarily designed).

Copper (T.D. 45878, 50158, 55977) articles classifiable under the provisions of Chapter 74, HTSUS—A statement of the weight of articles of copper, and a statement of percentage of copper content and all other elements—by weight—of articles classifiable according to copper content.

Copper ores and concentrates (T.D. 45878, 50158, 55977) classifiable in heading 2603, and subheadings 2620.19.60, 2620.20.00, 2620.30.00, and heading 7401—Statement of the percentage by weight of the copper content and any other metallic elements.

Cotton fabrics classifiable under the following HTSUS headings: 5208, 5209, 5210, 5211, and 5212—(1) Marks on shipping packages; (2) Numbers on shipping packages; (3) Customer's call number, if any; (4) Exact width of the merchandise; (5) Detailed description of the merchandise; trade name, if any; whether bleached, unbleached, printed, composed of yarns of different color, or dyed; if composed of cotton and other materials, state the percentage of each component material by weight; (6) Number of single threads per square centimeter (All ply yarns must be counted in accordance with the number of single threads contained in the yarn; to illustrate: a cloth containing 100 two-ply yarns in one square centimeter must be reported as 200 single threads); (7) Exact weight per square meter in grams; (8) Average yarn number use this formula:

$$\frac{100 \times \text{(Total Single Yarns Per Square Centimeter)}}{\text{(Number of Grams Per Square Meter}}$$

(9) Yarn size or sizes in the warp; (10) Yarn size or sizes in the filling; (11) Specify whether the yarns are combed or carded; (12) Number of colors or kinds (different yarn sizes or materials) in the filling; (13) Specify whether the fabric is napped or not napped; and (14) Specify the type of weave, for example, plain, twill, sateen, oxford, etc., and (15) Specify the type of machine on which woven: if with Jacquard (Jacq), if with Swivel (Swiv), if with Lappet (Lpt.), if with Dobby (Dobby).

Cotton raw See § 151.82 of this chapter for additional information required on invoices.

Cotton waste (T.D. 50044)—(1) The name by which the cotton waste is known, such as "cotton card strips"; "cotton comber waste"; "cotton lap waste"; "cotton sliver waste"; "cotton roving waste"; "cotton fly waste"; etc.; (2) Whether the length of the cotton staple forming any cotton card strips covered by the invoice is less than 3.016 centimeters ($1^3/_{16}$ inches) or is 3.016 centimeters ($1^3/_{16}$ inches) or more.

Earthenware or crockeryware composed of a nonvitrified absorbent body (including white granite and semiporcelain earthenware and cream-colored ware, stoneware, and terra cotta, but not including common brown, gray, red, or yellow earthenware), embossed or plain; common salt-glazed stoneware; stoneware or earthenware crucibles; Rockingham earthenware; china, porcelain, or other vitrified wares, composed of a vitrified nonabsorbent body which, when broken, shows a vitrified, vitreous, semi-vitrified, or semivitreous fracture; and bisque or parian ware (T.D. 53236)—(1) If in sets, the kinds of articles in each set in the shipment and the quantity of each kind of article in each set in the shipment; (2) The exact maximum diameter, expressed in centimeters, of each size of all plates in the shipment; (3) The unit value for each style and size of plate, cup, saucer, or other separate piece in the shipment.

Fish or fish livers (T.D. 50724, 49640, 55977) imported in airtight containers classifiable under Chapter 3, HTSUS—(1) Statement whether the articles contain an oil, fat, or grease, (2) The name and quantity of any such oil, fat, or grease.

Footwear, classifiable in headings 6401 through 6405 of the HTSUS—

1. Manufacturer's style number.

2. Importer's style and/or stock number.

3. Percent by area of external surface area of upper (excluding reinforcements and accessories) which is:

Leather	a. _____	%
Composition leather	b. _____	%
Rubber and/or plastics	c. _____	%
Textile materials	d. _____	%
Other (give separate	e. _____	%
percent for each	f. _____	%
type of material)		

4. Percent by area of external surface area of outersole (excluding reinforcements and accessories) which is:

Leather	a. _____	%
Composition leather	b. _____	%
Rubber and/or plastics	c. _____	%
Textile materials	d. _____	%
Other (give separate	e. _____	%
percent for each	f. _____	%
type of material)		

You may skip this section if you choose to answer *all* questions A through Z below:

I. If 3(a) is larger than any other percent in 3 and if 4(a) is larger than any other percent in 4, answer questions F, G, L, M, O, Q, R, S, and X.

II. If 3(a) is larger than any other percent in 3 and if 4(c) is larger than any other percent in 4, answer questions F, G, L, M, N, O, Q, S and X.

III. If 3(a) plus 3(b) is larger than any single percent in 3 and 4(d), 4(e) or 4(f) is larger than any other percent in 4, stop.

IV. If 3(c) is larger than any other percent in 3 and if 4(a) or 4(b) is larger than any other percent in 4, stop.

V. If 3(c) is larger than any other percent in 3 and if 4(c) is larger than any other percent in 4, answer questions B, E, F, G, H, J, K, L, M, N, O, P, T and W.

VI. If 3(d) is larger than any other percent in 3 and if 4(a) plus 4(b) is greater than any single percent in 4, answer questions C and D.

VII. If 3(d) is larger than any other percent in 3 and if 4(c) is larger than any single percent in 4, answer questions A, C, J, K, M, N, P and T.

VIII. If 3(d) is larger than any other percent in 3 and if 4(d) is larger than any other percent in 4, answer questions U, Y and Z.

IX. If the article is made of paper, answer questions V and Z.

If the article does not meet any of the conditions I through IX above, answer all questions A through Z, below.

A. Percent of external surface area of upper (including leather reinforcements and accessories).

Which is leather _____ %

B. Percent by area of external surface area of upper (including all reinforcements and accessories).

Which is rubber _____ and/or plastics _____ %

C. Percent by weight of rubber and/or plastics is _____ %

D. Percent by weight of textile materials plus rubber and/or plastics is _____ %

E. Is it waterproof?

F. Does it have a protective metal toe cap?

G. Will it cover the wearer's ankle bone?

H. Will it cover the wearer's knee cap?

I. [Reserved.]

J. Is it designed to be a protection against water, oil, grease, or chemicals or cold or inclement weather?

K. Is it a slip-on?

L. Is it a downhill or cross-country ski boot?

M. Is it serious sports footwear other than ski boots? (Chapter 64 subheading note defines sports footwear.)

N. Is it a tennis, basketball, gym, or training shoe or the like?

O. Is it made on a base or platform of wood?

P. Does it have open toes or open heels?

Q. Is it made by the (lipped insole) welt construction?

R. Is it made by the turned construction?

S. Is it worn exclusively by men, boys or youths?

T. Is it made by an exclusively adhesive construction?

U. Are the fibers of the upper, by weight, predominately vegetable fibers?

V. Is it disposable, i.e., intended for one-time use?

W. Is it a "Zori"?

X. Is the leather in the upper pigskin?

Y. Are the sole and upper made of wool felt?

Z. Is there a line of demarcation between the outer sole and upper?

The information requested above may be furnished on CF 5523 or other appropriate format by the exporter, manufacturer or shipper.

Also, the following information must be furnished by the importer or his authorized agent if classification is claimed under one of the subheadings below, as follows:

If subheading 6401.99.80, 6402.19.10, 6402.30.30, 6402.91.40, 6402.99.15, 6402.99.30, 6404.11.40, 6404.11.60, 6404.19.35, 6404.19.40, or 6404.19.60 is claimed:

Does the shoe have a foxing or foxing-like band? If so, state its material(s).

Does the sole overlap the upper other than just at the front of the toe and/or at the back of the heel?

Definitions for some of the terms used in Question A to Z above: For the purpose of this section, the following terms have the approximate definitions below. If either a more complete definition or a decision as to its application to a particular article is needed, the maker or importer of record (or the agent of either) should contact Customs prior to entry of the article.

a. In an exclusively adhesive construction, all of the pieces of the bottom would separate from the upper or from each other if all adhesives, cements, and glues were dissolved. It includes shoes in which the pieces of the upper are stitched to each other, but not to any part of the bottom. Examples include:

1. Vulcanized construction footwear;

2. Simultaneous molded construction footwear;

3. Molded footwear in which the upper and the bottom is one piece of molded rubber or plastic, and

4. Footwear in which staples, rivets, stitching, or any of the methods above are either primary or even just extra or auxiliary, even though adhesive is a major part of the reason the bottom will not separate from the upper.

b. Composition leather is made by binding together leather fibers or small pieces of natural leather. It does not include imitation leathers not based on natural leather.

c. Leather is the tanned skin of any animal from which the fur or hair has been removed. Tanned skins coated or laminated with rubber and/or plastics are ''leather'' only if leather gives the material its essential character.

d. A Line of Demarcation exists if one can indicate where the sole ends and the upper begins. For example, knit booties do not normally have a line of demarcation.

e. Men's, boy's and youth's sizes cover footwear of American youths size 11½ and larger for males, and does not include footwear commonly worn by both sexes. If more than 4% of the shoes sold in a given size will be worn by females, that size is ''commonly worn by both sexes.''

f. Footwear is designed to *protect* against water, oil or cold or inclement weather only if it is substantially more of a protection against those items than the usual shoes of that type. For example, a leather oxford will clearly keep your feet warmer and drier than going barefoot, but they are not a protection in this sense. On the other hand, the snow-jogger is the protective version of the nonprotective jogging shoe.

g. Rubber and/or plastics includes any textile material visibly coated (or covered) externally with one or both of those materials.

h. Slip-on includes:
1. A boot which must be pulled on.
2. Footwear with elastic cores which must be stretched to get it on, but not a separate piece of elasticized fabric which forms a full circle around the foot or ankle.

i. Sports footwear includes only:
1. Footwear which is designed for a sporting activity and has, or has provision for, the attachment of spikes, sprigs, cleats, stops, clips, bars or the like;
2. Skating boots (without skates attached), ski boots and cross-country ski footwear, wrestling boots, boxing boots and cycling shoes.

J. Tennis shoes, basketball shoes, gym shoes, training shoes and the like cover athletic footwear other than sports footwear, whether or not principally used for such athletic games or purposes.

k. Textile materials are made from cotton, other vegetable fibers, wool, hair, silk or man-made fibers. Note: Cork, wood, cardboard and leather are not textile materials.

l. In turned construction, the upper is stitched to the leather sole wrong side out and the shoe is then turned right side out.

m. Vegetable fibers include cotton, flax and ramie, but does not include either rayon or plaiting materials such as rattan or wood strips.

n. Waterproof footwear includes footwear designed to protect against penetration by water or other liquids, whether or not such footwear is primarily designed for such purposes.

o. Welt footwear means footwear construction with a welt, which extends around the edge of the outer sole, and in which the welt and shoe upper are sewed to a lip on the surface of the insole, and the outer sole of which is sewed or cemented to the welt.

p. A zori has an upper consisting only of straps or thongs of molded rubber or plastic. This upper is assembled to a formed rubber or plastic sole by means of plugs.

Fur products and furs (T.D. 53064)—(1) Name or names (as set forth in the Fur Products Name Guide (16 CFR 301.0) of the animal or animals that produced the fur, and such qualifying statements as may be required pursuant to § 7(c) of the Fur Products Labeling Act (15 U.S.C. 69e(c)); (2) A statement that the fur product contains or is composed of used fur, when such is the fact; (3) A statement that the fur product contains or is composed of bleached, dyed, or otherwise artificially colored fur, when such is the fact; (4) A statement that the fur product is composed in whole or in substantial part of paws, tails, bellies, or waste fur, when such is the fact; (5) Name and address of the manufacturer of the fur product; (6) Name of the country of origin of the furs or those contained in the fur product.

Glassware and other glass products (T.D. 53079, 55977)— Classifiable under Chapter 70, HTSUS—Statement of the separate value of each component article in the set.

Gloves—classifiable in subheadings 6116.10.20 and 6216.00.20— Statement as to whether or not the article has been covered with plastics on both sides.

Grain or grain and screenings (T.D. 51284)—Statement on Customs invoices for cultivated grain or grain and screenings that no screenings are included with the grain, or, if there are screenings included, the percentage of the shipment which consists of screenings commingled with the principal grain.

Handkerchiefs—(1) State the exact dimensions (length and width) of the merchandise; (2) If of cotton indicate whether the handkerchief is hemmed and whether it contains lace or embroidery.

Hats or headgear—(1) If classifiable under subheading 6502.00.40 or 6502.00.60, HTSUS—Statement as to whether or not the article has been bleached or colored; (2) If classifiable under subheading 6502.00.20 through 6502.00.60 or 6504.00.30 through 6504.00.90, HTSUS—Statement as to whether or not the article is sewed or not sewed, exclusive of any ornamentation or trimming.

Hosiery—(1) Indicate whether a single yarn measures less than 67 decitex. (2) Indicate whether the hosiery is full length, knee length, or less than knee length. (3) Indicate whether it contains lace or net.

Iron or Steel classifiable in Chapter 72 or headings 7301 to 7307, HTSUS (T.D. 53092, 55977)—Statement of the percentages by weight of carbon and any metallic elements contained in the articles, in the form of a mill analysis or mill test certificate.

Iron oxide (T.D. 49989, 50107)—For iron oxide to which a reduced rate of duty is applicable, a statement of the method of preparation of the oxide, together with the patent number, if any.

Machines, equipment and apparatus—Chapters 84 and 85, HTSUS— A statement as to the use or method of operation of each type of machine.

Machine parts (T.D. 51616)—Statement specifying the kind of machine for which the parts are intended, or if this is not known to the shipper, the kinds of machines for which the parts are suitable.

Machine tools: (1) Heading 8456 through 8462—machine tools covered by these headings equipped with a CNC (Computer Numerical Control) or the facings (electrical interface) for a CNC must state so; (2) heading 8458 through 8463—machine tools covered by these headings if used or rebuilt must state so; (3) subheading 8456.30.10—EDM: (Electrical Discharge Machines) if a Traveling Wire (Wire Cut) type must state so. Wire EDM's use a copper or brass wire for the electrode; (4) subheading 8457.10.0010 through 8457.10.0050—Machining Centers. Must state whether or not they have an ATC (Automatic Tool Changer). Vertical spindle machine centers with an ATC must also indicate the Y-travel; (5) subheadings 8458.11.0030 through 8458.11.00.90—horizontal lathes: numerically controlled. Must indicate the rated HP (or KW rating) of the main spindle motor. Use the continuous rather than 30-minute rating.

Madeira embroideries (T.D. 49988)—(1) With respect to the materials used, furnish: (a) country of production; (b) width of the material in the piece; (c) name of the manufacturer; (d) kind of material, indicating manufacturer's quality number; (e) landed cost of the material used in each item; (f) date of the order; (g) date of the invoice; (h) invoice unit value in the currency of the purchase; (i) discount from purchase price allowed, if any, (2) with respect to the finished embroidered articles, furnish: (a) manufacturer's name, design number, and quality number; (b) importer's design number, if any; (c) finished size; (d) number of embroidery points per unit of quantity; (e) total for overhead and profit added in arriving at the price or value of the merchandise covered by the invoice.

Motion-picture films—(1) Statement of footage, title, and subject matter of each film; (2) declaration of shipper, cameraman, or other person with knowledge of the facts identifying the films with the invoice and stating that the basic films were to the best of his knowledge and belief exposed abroad and returned for use as newsreel; (3) declaration of importer that he believes the films entered by him are the ones covered by the preceding declaration and that the films are intended for use as newsreel.

Paper classifiable in Chapter 48—Invoices covering paper shall contain the following information, or will be accompanied by specification sheets containing such information:

(1) weight of paper in grams per square meter; (2) thickness, in micrometers (microns); (3) if imported in rectangular sheets, length and width sheets, in cm; (4) if imported in strips, or rolls, the width, in cm. In the case of rolls, the diameter of rolls in cm; (5) whether the paper is coated or impregnated, and with wha· materials; (6) weight of coating, in grams per square meter; (7) percentage by weight of the total fiber content consisting of wood fibers contained by a mechanical process, chemical sulfate or soda process, chemical sulfite process, or semi-chemical process, as appropriate; (8) commercial designation, as "writing", "cover", "drawing", "Bristol", "newsprint", etc.; (9) ash content; (10) color; (11) glaze, or finish; (12) Mullen bursting strength, and Mullen index; (13) stretch factor, in machine direction and in cross direction; (14) tear and tensile readings; in machine direction, in cross direction, and in machine direction plus cross direction; (15) identification of fibers as "hardwood" where appropriate; (16) crush resistance; (17) brightness; (18) smoothness; (19) if bleached, whether bleached uniformly throughout the mass; (20) whether embossed, perforated, creped or crinkled.

Plastic plates, sheets, film, foil and strip of headings 3920 and 3921—
(1) Statement as to whether the plastic is cellular or noncellular; (2)

specification of the type of plastic: (3) indication of whether or not flexible and whether combined with textile or other material.

Printed matter classifiable in Chapter 49—Printed matter entered in the following headings shall have, on or with the invoices covering such matter, the following information: (1) *Heading 4901*—(a) whether the books are: dictionaries, encyclopedias, textbooks, bound newspapers or journals or periodicals, directories, bibles or other prayer books, technical, scientific or professional books, art or pictorial books, or "other" books; (b) if "other" books, whether hardbound or paperbound; (c) if "other" books, paperbound, other than "rack size": number of pages (excluding covers). (2) *Heading 4902*—(a) whether the journal or periodical appears at least four times a week. If the journal or periodical appears other than at least four times a week, whether it is a newspaper supplement printed by a gravure process, is a newspaper, business or professional journal or periodical, or other than these; (3) *Heading 4904*—whether the printed or manuscript music is sheet music, not bound (except by stapling or folding); (4) *Heading 4905*—(a) whether globes, or not; (b) if not globes, whether in book form, or not; (c) in any case, whether or not in relief; (5) *Heading 4908*—Whether or not vitrifiable; (6) *Heading 4904*—whether post cards, greeting cards, or other; (7) *Heading 4910*—(a) whether or not printed on paper by a lithographic process; (b) if printed on paper by a lithographic process, the thickness of the paper, in mm; (8) *Subheading 4911.91*—(a) whether or not printed over 20 years at time of importation; (b) if not printed over 20 years at time of importation, whether suitable for use in the production of articles of heading 4901; (c) if not printed over 20 years at time of importation, and not suitable for use in the production of articles of heading 4901, whether the merchandise is lithographs on paper or paperboard; (d) if lithographs on paper or paperboard, under the terms of the immediately preceding description, thickness of the paper or paperboard, and whether or not posters; (e) in any case, whether or not posters; (f) in any case, whether or not photographic negatives or positives on transparent bases; (g) *Subheading 4911.99*—If not carnets, or parts thereof, in English or French, whether or not printed on paper in whole or in part by a lithographic process.

Pulp classifiable in Chapter 47—(1) Invoices covering chemical woodpulp, dissolving grades, in *Heading 4702* shall state the insoluble fraction (as a percentage) after 1 hour in a caustic soda solution containing 18% sodium hydroxide (NaOH) at 20° C; (2) *Subheading 4702.00.0020*—Pulp entered under this subheading shall in addition contain on or with the invoice the ash content as a percentage by weight.

Refrigeration equipment (1) Refrigerator-freezers classifiable under subheading 8418.10.00 and (2) refrigerators classifiable under 8418.21.00—(a) statement as to whether they are compression or absorption type; (b) statement of their refrigerated volume in liters; (3) freezers classifiable under subheading 8418.30.00 and 8418.40.00—statement as to whether they are chest or upright type; (4) liquid chilling refrigerating units classifiable under subheading 8418.69.0045 through 8418.69.0060—statement as to whether they are centrifugal open-type, centrifugal hermetic-type, absorption-type or reciprocating type.

Rolling mills—Subheading 8455.30.0005 through 8455.30.0085. Rolls for rolling mills: Indicate the composition of the roll—gray iron, cast steel or other—and the weight of each roll.

Rubber Products of Chapter 40—(1) Statement as to whether combined with textile or other material; (2) statement whether the rubber is cellular or noncellular, unvulcanized or vulcanized, and if vulcanized, whether hard rubber or other than hard rubber.

Screenings or scalpings of grains or seeds (T.D. 51096)—
(1) Whether the commodity is the product of a screening process; (2) if so, whether any cultivated grains have been added to such

commodity; (3) If any such grains have been added, the kind and percentage of each.

Textile fiber products (T.D. 55095—(1) The constituent fiber or combination of fibers in the textile fiber product, designating with equal prominence each natural or manufactured fiber in the textile fiber product by its generic name in the order of predominance by the weight thereof if the weight of such fiber is 5 per cent or more of the total fiber weight of the product; (2) percentage of each fiber present, by weight, in the total fiber content of the textile fiber product; (3) the name, or other identification issued and registered by the Federal Trade Commission, of the manufacturer of the product or one or more persons subject to § 3 of the Textile Fiber Products Identification Act (15 U.S.C. 70a) with respect to such product; (4) the name of the country where processed or manufactured. *See also* "Wearing Apparel" below.

Tires and Tubes for tires , of rubber or plastics—(1) Specify the kind of vehicle for which the tire is intended, i.e. airplane, bicycle, passenger car, on-the-highway light or heavy truck or bus, motorcycle; (2) if designed for tractors provided for in subheading 8701.90.10, or for agricultural or horticultural machinery or implements provided for in Chapter 84 or in subheading 8716.80.10, designate whether the tire is new, recapped, or used; pneumatic or solid; (3) indicate whether the tube is designed for tires provided for in subheading 4011.91.10, 4011.99.10, 4012.10.20, or 4012.20.20.

Tobacco (including tobacco in its natural state) (T.D. 44854, 45871)—(1) Specify in detail the character of the tobacco in each bale by giving (a) country and province of origin, (b) year of production, (c) grade or grades in each bale, (d) number of carrots or pounds of each grade if more than one grade is packed in a bale, (e) the time when, place where, and person from whom purchased, (f) price paid or to be paid for each bale or package, or price for the vega or lot if purchased in bulk, or if obtained otherwise than by purchase, state the actual market value per bale; (2) if an invoice covers or includes bales of tobacco which are part of a vega or lot purchased in bulk, the invoice must contain or be accompanied by a full description of the vega or lot purchased; or if such description has been furnished with a previous importation, the date and identity of such shipment; (3) packages or bales containing only filler leaf shall be invoiced as filler; when containing filler and wrapper but not more than 35 percent of wrapper, they shall be invoiced as mixed; and when containing more than 35 percent of wrapper, they shall be invoiced as wrapper.

Watches and watch movements classifiable under Chapter 91 of the HTSUS—For all commercial shipments of such articles, there shall be required to be shown on the invoice, or on a separate sheet attached to and constituting a part of the invoice, such information as will reflect with respect to each group, type, or model, the following:

(A) For watches, a thorough description of the composition of the watch cases, the bracelets, bands or straps, the commercial description (ebauche caliber number, ligne size and number of jewels) of the movements contained in the watches, and the type of battery (manufacturer's name and reference number), if the watch is battery-operated.

(B) For watch movements, the commercial description (ebauche caliber number, ligne size and number of jewels). If battery-operated, t'.e type of battery (manufacturer's name and reference number).

(C) The name of the manufacturer of the exported watch movements and the name of the country in which the movements were manufactured.

Wearing apparel —(a) All invoices for textile wearing apparel should indicate a component material breakdown in percentages by weight for all component fibers present in the entire garment, as well as separate breakdowns of the fibers in the (outer) shell (exclusive of linings, cuffs, waistbands, collars and other trimmings) and in the lining; (2) for garments which are constructed of more than one component or material (combination of knits and not knit fabric or combinations of knit and/or not knit fabric with leather, fur, plastic including vinyl, etc.), the invoice must show a fiber breakdown in percentages by weight for each separate textile material in the garment and a breakdown in percentages by weight for each nontextile material for the entire garment; (3) for woven garments—Indicate whether the fabric is yarn dyed and whether there are "two or more colors in the warp and/or filling"; (4) for all-white T-shirts and singlets—Indicate whether or not the garment contains pockets, trim, or embroidery; (5) for mufflers—State the exact dimensions (length and width) of the merchandise.

Wood products—(1) Wood sawed or chipped lengthwise, sliced or peeled, whether or not planed, sanded, or finger-jointed, of a thickness exceeding 6 mm (lumber), classifiable under Chapter 44, heading 4407, HTSUS, and wood continuously shaped along any of its edges or faces, whether or not planed, sanded or finger-jointed; coniferous: Subheading 4409.10.90 and nonconiferous: Subheading 4409.20.90, HTSUS, and dutiable on the basis of cubic meters—
Quantity in cubic meter (m) before dressing; (2) fiberboard of wood or other ligneous materials whether or not bonded with resins or other organic substances, under Chapter 44, Heading 4411, HTSUS, and classifiable according to its density—density in grams per cubic centimeter (cm); (3) plywood consisting solely of sheets of wood, classifiable under Chapter 44, Subheading 4412.11, 4412.12, and 4412.19, HTSUS, and classifiable according to the thickness of the wood sheets—thickness of each ply in millimeter (mm);

Wool and hair —See § 151.62 of this chapter for additional information required on invoices.

Wool products, except carpets, rugs, mats, and upholsteries, and wool products made more than 20 years before importation (T.D. 50388, 51019)—(1) The percentage of the total fiber weight of the wool product, exclusive of ornamentation not exceeding 5 per cent of said total fiber weight, of (a) wool; (b) reprocessed wool; (c) reused wool; (d) each fiber other than wool if said percentage by weight of such fiber is 5 per cent or more; and (e) the aggregate of all other fibers; (2) the maximum percentage of the total weight of the wool product, of any nonfibrous loading, filling, or adulterating matter; and (3) the name of the manufacturer of the wool product, except when such product consists of mixed wastes, residues, and similar merchandise obtained from several suppliers or unknown sources.

Woven fabric of man-made fibers in headings 5407, 5408, 5512, 5513, 5514, 5515, 5516—
(1) State the exact width of the fabric.
(2) Provide a detailed description of the merchandise, (trade name, if any).
(3) Indicate whether bleached, unbleached, dyed, of yarns of different colors and/or printed.
(4) If composed of more than one material, list percentage by weight in each.
(5) Identify the man-made fibers as artificial or synthetic, filament or staple, and state whether the yarns are high tenacity. Specify the number of turns per meter in each yarn.
(6) Specify yarn sizes in warp and filling.
(7) Specify how the fabric is woven (plain weave, twill, sateen, dobby, jacquard, swivel, lappet, etc.).

(8) Indicate the number of single threads per square centimeter in both warp and filling.

(9) Supply the weight per square meter in grams.

(10) Provide the average yarn number using this formula:
$$\frac{100 \times \text{number of single threads per square centimeter}}{(\text{number of grams per square meter})}.$$

(11) For spun yarns, specify whether textured or not textured.

(12) For filament yarns, specify whether textured or not textured.

Yarns—(1) All yarn invoices should show: (a) fiber content by weight; (b) whether single or plied; (c) whether or not put up for retail sale (See Section XI, Note 4, HTSUS);

(d) whether or not intended for use as sewing thread.

(2) If chief weight of silk—show whether spun or filament.

(3) If chief weight of cotton—show:
(a) whether combed or uncombed
(b) metric number (mn)
(c) whether bleached and/or mercerized.

(4) If chief weight of man-made fiber—show:
(a) whether filament, or spun, or a combination of filament and spun
(b) If a combination of filament and spun—give percentage of filament and spun by weight.

(5) If chief weight of filament man-made fiber—show:
(a) whether high tenacity (See Section XI, note 6 HTSUS)
(b) whether monofilament, multifilament or strip
(c) whether texturized
(d) yarn number in decitex
(e) number of turns per meter
(f) for monofilaments—show cross-sectional dimension in millimeters
(g) for strips—show the width of the strip in millimeters (measure in folded or twisted condition if so imported).

Special Summary Steel Invoice (1) A Special Summary Steel Invoice (Customs Form 5520) shall be filed in duplicate at the time of filing the entry summary for each shipment determined by the district director to have an aggregate purchase price of $10,000 or over or, if from a contiguous country, of $5,000 or over (including all expenses incident to placing the merchandise in conditioned packed ready for shipment to the United States), and containing any of the articles of steel listed in paragraph (b)(2) of this section. In addition to the information required by § 141.86, the Special Summary Steel Invoice shall set forth the following: (T.D.'s 78-53, 79-79, 79-221, 81-291).

(A) The date of agreement of the final sales price for the shipment.

(B) A description of, and the additional price charged for extras, other than width and length, with extras described in terms understood in the U.S. market.

(C) American Iron and Steel Institute (AISI) category.

(D) The base price for each steel category on which the total sales price was based.

(E) The name of the producer, the importer, and the price paid by the first unrelated purchaser in the United States, if that price is available at the time of filing the entry summary. One or more continuation sheets may be used to supply this information, if necessary. (T.D. 79-221.)

(F) Identification, by number, of any applicable standards, such as American Society for Testing and Materials (ASTM), American Pipe Institute (API), or other generally accepted standards.

(G) Name of the country where the steel was poured or cast, and, if any other processing occurred outside of the pouring or casting country, list each country where processing occurred along with a description of the processing, and each date of export from each country.

(2) The following articles of steel, listed by AISI category and product name, are subject to the special invoice requirements of § 141.89(b)(1):

(1) Ingots, blooms, billets, slabs, etc.

(2) Wire rods.

(3) Structural shapes, plain 76mm and over.

(4) Sheet piling.

(5) Plates.

(6) Rail and track accessories.

(7) Wheels and axles.

(8) Concrete reinforcing bars.

(9) Bar shapes under 76 mm.

(10) Bars, hot rolled, carbon.

(11) Bars, hot rolled, alloy.

(12) Bars, cold finished.

(13) Hollow drill steel.

(14) Welded pipe and tubing.

(15) Other pipe and tubing.

(16) Round and shaped wire.

(17) Flat wire.

Items or classes of goods may be added to or removed from the list from time to time.

3 customs valuation

TARIFF ACT OF 1930

"SEC. 402, VALUE. [19 U.S.C. 1401a]

"(a) IN GENERAL.—(1) Except as otherwise specifically provided for in this Act, imported merchandise shall be appraised, for the purposes of this Act, on the basis of the following:

"(A) The transaction value provided for under subsection (b).

"(B) The transaction value of identical merchandise provided for under subsection (c), if the value referred to in subparagraph (A) cannot be determined, or can be determined but cannot be used by reason of subsection (b)(2).

"(C) The transaction value of similar merchandise provided for under subsection (c), if the value referred to in subparagraph (B) cannot be determined.

"(D) The deductive value provided for under subsection (d), if the value referred to in subparagraph (C) cannot be determined and if the importer does not request alternative valuation under Paragraph (2).

"(E) The computed value provided for under subsection (e), if the value referred to in subparagraph (D) cannot be determined.

"(F) The value provided for under subsection (f), if the value referred to in subparagraph (E) cannot be determined.

"(2) If the value referred to in paragraph (1)(C) cannot be determined with respect to imported merchandise, the merchandise shall be appraised on the basis of the computed value provided for under paragraph (1)(E), rather than the deductive value provided for under paragraph (1)(D), if the importer makes a request to that effect to the customs officer concerned within such time as the Secretary shall prescribe. If the computed value of the merchandise cannot subsequently be determined, the merchandise may not be appraised on the basis of the value referred to in paragraph (1)(F) unless the deductive value of the merchandise cannot be determined under paragraph (1)(D).

"(3) Upon written request therefor by the importer of merchandise, and subject to provisions of law regarding the disclosure of information, the customs officer concerned shall provide the importer with a written explanation of how the value of that merchandise was determined under this section.

"(b) TRANSACTION VALUE OF IMPORTED MERCHANDISE.—(1) The transaction value of imported merchandise is the price actually paid or payable for the merchandise when sold for exportation to the United States, plus amounts equal to—

"(A) the packing costs incurred by the buyer with respect to the imported merchandise;

"(B) any selling commission incurred by the buyer with respect to the imported merchandise;

"(C) the value, apportioned as appropriate, of any assist;

"(D) any royalty or license fee related to the imported merchandise that the buyer is required to pay, directly or indirectly, as a condition of the sale of the imported merchandise for exportation to the United States; and

"(E) the proceeds of any subsequent resale, disposal, or use of the imported merchandise that accrue, directly or indirectly, to the seller.

The price actually paid or payable for imported merchandise shall be increased by the amounts attributable to the items (and no others) described in subparagraphs (A) through (E) only to the extent that each such amount (i) is not otherwise included within the price actually paid or payable; and (ii) is based on sufficient information. If sufficient information is not available, for any reason, with respect to any amount referred to in the preceding sentence, the transaction value of the imported merchandise concerned shall be treated, for purposes of this section, as one that cannot be determined.

"(2)(A) The transaction value of imported merchandise determined under paragraph (1) shall be the appraised value of that merchandise for the purposes of this Act only if—

"(i) there are no restrictions on the disposition or use of the imported merchandise by the buyer other than restrictions that—

"(I) are imposed or required by law,

"(II) limit the geographical area in which the merchandise may be resold, or

"(III) do not substantially affect the value of the merchandise;

"(ii) the sale of, or the price actually paid or payable for, the imported merchandise is not subject to any condition or consideration for which a value cannot be determined with respect to the imported merchandise;

"(iii) no part of the proceeds of any subsequent resale, disposal, or use of the imported merchandise by the buyer will accrue directly or indirectly to the seller, unless an appropriate adjustment therefor can be made under paragraph (1)(E); and

"(iv) the buyer and seller are not related, or the buyer and seller are related but the transaction value is acceptable, for purposes of this subsection, under subparagraph (B).

"(B) The transaction value between a related buyer and seller is acceptable for the purposes of this subsection if an examination of the circumstances of the sale of the imported merchandise indicates that the relationship between such buyer and seller did not influence the price actually paid or payable; or if the transaction value of the imported merchandise closely approximates—

Amended by P.L. 96–490, effective 1/1/81.

"(i) the transaction value of identical merchandise, or of similar merchandise, in sales to unrelated buyers in the United States; or

"(ii) the deductive value or computed value for identical merchandise or similar merchandise;

but, only if each value referred to in clause (i) or (ii) that is used for comparison relates to merchandise that was exported to the United States at or about the same time as the imported merchandise.

"(C) In applying the values used for comparison purposes under subparagraph (B), there shall be taken into account differences with respect to the sales involved (if such differences are based on sufficient information whether supplied by the buyer or otherwise available to the customs officer concerned) in—

"(i) commercial levels;

"(ii) quantity levels;

"(iii) the costs, commissions, values, fees, and proceeds described in paragraph (1); and

"(iv) the costs incurred by the seller in sales in which he and the buyer are not related that are not incurred by the seller in sales in which he and the buyer are related.

"(3) The transaction value of imported merchandise does not include any of the following, if identified separately from the price actually paid or payable and from any cost or other item referred to in paragraph (1):

"(A) Any reasonable cost or charge that is incurred for—

"(i) the construction, erection, assembly, or maintenance of, or the technical assistance provided with respect to, the merchandise after its importation into the United States; or

"(ii) the transportation of the merchandise after such importation.

"(B) The customs duties and other Federal taxes currently payable on the imported merchandise by reason of its importation, and any Federal excise tax on, or measured by the value of, such merchandise for which vendors in the United States are ordinarily liable.

"(4) For purposes of this subsection—

"(A) The term 'price actually paid or payable' means the total payment (whether direct or indirect, and exclusive of any costs, charges, or expenses incurred for transportation, insurance, and related services incident to the international shipment of the merchandise from the country of exportation to the place of importation in the United States) made, or to be made, for imported merchandise by the buyer to, or for the benefit of, the seller.

"(B) Any rebate of, or other decrease in, the price actually paid or payable that is made or otherwise effected between the buyer and seller after the date of the importation of the merchandise into the United States shall be disregarded in determining the transaction value under paragraph (1).

"(c) TRANSACTION VALUE OF IDENTICAL MERCHANDISE AND SIMILAR MERCHANDISE.—(1) The transaction value of identical merchandise, or of similar merchandise, is the transaction value (acceptable as the appraised value for purposes of this Act under subsection (b) but adjusted under paragraph (2) of this subsection) of imported merchandise that is—

"(A) with respect to the merchandise being appraised, either identical merchandise or similar merchandise, as the case may be; and

"(B) exported to the United States at or about the time that the merchandise being appraised is exported to the United States.

"(2) Transaction values determined under this subsection shall be based on sales of identical merchandise or similar merchandise, as the case may be, at the same commercial level and in substantially the same quantity as the sales of the merchandise being appraised. If no such sale is found, sales of identical merchandise or similar merchandise at either a different commercial level or in different quantities, or both, shall be used, but adjusted to take account of any such difference. Any adjustment made under this paragraph shall be based on sufficient information. If in applying this paragraph with respect to any imported merchandise, two or more transaction values for identical merchandise, or for similar merchandise, are determined, such imported merchandise shall be appraised on the basis of the lower or lowest of such values.

"(d) DEDUCTIVE VALUE.—(1) For purposes of this subsection, the term 'merchandise concerned' means the merchandise being appraised, identical merchandise, or similar merchandise.

"(2)(A) The deductive value of the merchandise being appraised is whichever of the following prices (as adjusted under paragraph (3)) is appropriate depending upon when and in what condition the merchandise concerned is sold in the United States:

"(i) If the merchandise concerned is sold in the condition as imported at or about the date of importation of the merchandise being appraised, the price

Marginal notes:
"Price actually paid or payable."

"Merchandise concerned."

is the unit price at which the merchandise concerned is sold in the greatest aggregate quantity at or about such date.

"(ii) If the merchandise concerned is sold in the condition as imported but not sold at or about the date of importation of the merchandise being appraised, the price is the unit price at which the merchandise concerned is sold in the greatest aggregate quantity after the date of importation of the merchandise being appraised but before the close of the 90th day after the date of such importation.

"(iii) If the merchandise concerned was not sold in the condition as imported and not sold before the close of the 90th day after the date of importation of the merchandise being appraised, the price is the unit price at which the merchandise being appraised, after further processing, is sold in the greatest aggregate quantity before the 180th day after the date of such importation. This clause shall apply to appraisement of merchandise only if the importer so elects and notifies the customs officer concerned of that election within such time as shall be prescribed by the Secretary.

"(B) For purposes of subparagraph (A), the unit price at which merchandise is sold in the greatest aggregate quantity is the unit price at which such merchandise is sold to unrelated persons, at the first commercial level after importation (in cases to which subparagraph (A)(i) or (ii) applies) or after further processing (in cases to which subparagraph (A)(iii) applies) at which such sales take place, in a total volume that is (i) greater than the total volume sold at any other unit price, and (ii) sufficient to establish the unit price. Unit Price.

"(3)(A) The price determined under paragraph (2) shall be reduced by an amount equal to—

"(i) any commission usually paid or agreed to be paid, or the addition usually made for profit and general expenses, in connection with sales in the United States of imported merchandise that is of the same class or kind, regardless of the country of exportation as the merchandise concerned;

"(ii) the actual costs and associated costs of transportation and insurance incurred with respect to international shipments of the merchandise concerned from the country of exportation to the United States;

"(iii) The usual costs and associated costs of transportation and insurance incurred with respect to shipments of such merchandise from the place of importation to the place of delivery in the United States, if such costs are not included as a general expense under clause (i);

"(iv) the customs duties and other Federal taxes currently payable on the merchandise concerned by reason of its importation, and any Federal excise tax on, or measured by the value of, such merchandise for which vendors in the United States are ordinarily liable; and

"(v) (but only in the case of a price determined under paragraph (2)(A)(iii)) the value added by the processing of the merchandise after importation to the extent that the value is based on sufficient information relating to cost of such processing.

"(B) For purposes of applying paragraph (A)—

"(i) the deduction made for profits and general expenses shall be based upon the importer's profits and general expenses, unless such profits and general expenses are inconsistent with those reflected in sales in the United States of imported merchandise of the same class or kind, in which case the deduction shall be based on the usual profit and general expenses reflected in such sales, as determined from sufficient information; and

"(ii) any State or local tax imposed on the importer with respect to the sale of imported merchandise shall be treated as a general expense.

"(C) The price determined under paragraph (2) shall be increased (but only to the extent that such costs are not otherwise included) by an amount equal to the packing costs incurred by the importer or the buyer, as the case may be, with respect to the merchandise concerned.

"(D) For purposes of determining the deductive value of imported merchandise, any sale to a person who supplies any assist for use in connection with the production or sale for export of the merchandise concerned shall be disregarded.

"(e) COMPUTED VALUE.—(1) The computed value of imported merchandise is the sum of—

"(A) the cost or value of the materials and the fabrication and other processing of any kind employed in the production of the imported merchandise;

"(B) an amount for profit and general expenses equal to that usually reflected in sales of merchandise of the same class or kind as the imported merchandise that are made by the producers in the country of exportation for export to the United States;

"(C) any assist, if its value is not included under subparagraph (A) or (B); and

"(D) the packing costs.

"(2) For purposes of paragraph (1)—

"(A) the cost or value of materials under paragraph (1)(A) shall not include the amount of any internal tax imposed by the country of exportation that is directly applicable to the materials or their disposition if the tax is remitted or refunded upon the exportation of the merchandise in the production of which the materials were used; and

"(B) the amount for profit and general expenses under paragraph (1)(B) shall be based upon the producer's profits and expenses, unless the producer's profits and expenses are inconsistent with those usually reflected in sales of merchandise of the same class or kind as the imported merchandise that are made by producers in the country of exportation for export to the United States, in which case the amount under paragraph (1)(B) shall be based on the usual profit and general expenses of such producers in such sales, as determined from sufficient information.

"(f) VALUE IF OTHER VALUES CANNOT BE DETERMINED OR USED.— (1) If the value of imported merchandise cannot be determined, or otherwise used for the purposes of this Act, under subsections (b) through (e), the merchandise shall be appraised for the purposes of this Act on the basis of a value that is derived from the methods set forth in such subsections, with such methods being reasonably adjusted to the extent necessary to arrive at a value.

"(2) Imported merchandise may not be appraised, for the purposes of this Act, on the basis of— | *Imported merchandise appraisal.*

"(A) the selling price in the United States of merchandise produced in the United States;

"(B) a system that provides for the appraisement of imported merchandise at the higher of two alternative values;

"(C) the price of merchandise in the domestic market of the country of exportation;

"(D) a cost of production, other than a value determined under subsection (e) for merchandise that is identical merchandise or similar merchandise to the merchandise being appraised;

"(E) the price of merchandise for export to a country other than the United States;

"(F) minimum values for appraisement; or

"(G) arbitrary or fictitious values.

This paragraph shall not apply with respect to the ascertainment, determination, or estimation of foreign market value or United States price under title VII.

Ante, p. 150.

"(g) SPECIAL RULES.—(1) For purposes of this section, the persons specified in any of the following subparagraphs shall be treated as persons who are related:

"(A) Members of the same family, including brothers and sisters (whether by whole or half blood), spouse, ancestors, and lineal descendants.

"(B) Any officer or director of an organization and such organization.

"(C) Any officer or director of an organization and an officer or director of another organization, if each such individual is also an officer or director in the other organization.

"(D) Partners.

"(E) Employer and employee.

"(F) Any person directly or indirectly owning, controlling, or holding with power to vote, 5 percent or more of the outstanding voting stock or shares of any organization and such organization.

"(G) Two or more persons directly or indirectly controlling, controlled by, or under common control with, any person.

"(2) For purposes of this section, merchandise (including, but not limited to, identical merchandise and similar merchandise) shall be treated as being of the same class or kind as other merchandise if it is within a group or range of merchandise produced by a particular industry or industry sector.

"(3) For purposes of this section, information that is submitted by an importer, buyer, or producer in regard to the appraisement of merchandise may not be rejected by the customs officer concerned on the basis of the accounting method by which that information was prepared, if the preparation was in accordance with generally accepted accounting principles. The term 'generally accepted accounting principles' refers to any generally recognized consensus or substantial authoritative support regarding—

Generally accepted accounting principles.

"(A) which economic resources and obligations should be recorded as assets and liabilities;

"(B) which changes in assets and liabilities should be recorded;

"(C) how the assets and liabilities and changes in them should be measured;

"(D) what information should be disclosed and how it should be disclosed; and

"(E) which financial statements should be prepared.

The applicability of a particular set of generally accepted accounting principles will depend upon the basis on which the value of the merchandise is sought to be established.

"(h) DEFINITIONS.—As used in this section—

"(1)(A) The term 'assist' means any of the following if supplied directly or indirectly, and free of charge or at reduced cost, by the buyer of imported merchandise for use in connection with the production or the sale for export to the United States of the merchandise:

"(i) Materials, components, parts and similar items incorporated in the imported merchandise.

"(ii) Tools, dies, molds, and similar items used in the production of the imported merchandise.

"(iii) Merchandise consumed in the production of the imported merchandise.

"(iv) Engineering, development, artwork, design work, and plans and sketches that are undertaken elsewhere than in the United States and are necessary for the production of the imported merchandise.

"(B) No service or work to which subparagraph (A)(iv) applies shall be treated as an assist for purposes of this section if such service or work—

"(i) is performed by an individual who is domiciled within the United States;

"(ii) is performed by that individual while he is acting as an employee or agent of the buyer of the imported merchandise; and

"(iii) is incidental to other engineering, development, artwork, design work, or plans or sketches that are undertaken within the United States.

"(C) For purposes of this section, the following apply in determining the value of assists described in subparagraph (A)(iv):

"(i) The value of an assist that is available in the public domain is the cost of obtaining copies of the assist,

"(ii) If the production of an assist occurred in the United States and one or more foreign countries, the value of the assist is the value thereof that is added outside the United States.

"(2) The term 'identical merchandise' means—

"(A) merchandise that is identical in all respects to, and was produced in the same country and by the same person as, the merchandise being appraised; or

"(B) if merchandise meeting the requirements under subparagraph (A) cannot be found (or for purposes of applying subsection (b)(2)(B) (i), regardless of whether merchandise meeting such requirements can be found), merchandise that is identical in all respects to, and was produced in the same country as, but not produced by the same person as, the merchandise being appraised.

Such term does not include merchandise that incorporates or reflects any engineering, development, artwork, design work, or plan or sketch that—

"(I) was supplied free or at reduced cost by the buyer of the merchandise for use in connection with the production or the sale for export to the United States of the merchandise; and

"(II) is not an assist because undertaken within the United States.

"(3) The term 'packing costs' means the cost of all containers and coverings of whatever nature and of packing, whether for labor or materials, used in placing merchandise in condition, packed ready for shipment to the United States.

"(4) The term 'similar merchandise' means—

"(A) merchandise that—

"(i) was produced in the same country and by the same person as the merchandise being appraised,

"(ii) is like the merchandise being appraised in characteristics and component material, and

"(iii) is commercially interchangeable with the merchandise being appraised; or

"(B) if merchandise meeting the requirements under subparagraph (A) cannot be found (or for purposes of applying subsection (b)(2)(B)(i), regardless of whether merchandise meeting such requirements can be found), merchandise that—

"(i) was produced in the same country as, but not produced by the same person as, the merchandise being appraised, and

"(ii) meets the requirement set forth in subparagraph (A)(ii) and (iii).

Such term does not include merchandise that incorporates or reflects any engineering, development, artwork, design work, or plan or sketch that—

"(I) was supplied free or at reduced cost by the buyer of the merchandise for use in connection with the production or the sale for export to the United States of the merchandise; and

"(II) is not an assist because undertaken within the United States.

"(5) The term 'sufficient information', when required under this section for determining—

"(A) any amount—

"(i) added under subsection (b)(1) to the price actually paid or payable,

"(ii) deducted under subsection (d)(3) as profit or general expense or value from further processing, or

"(iii) added under subsection (e)(2) as profit or general expense;

"(B) any difference taken into account for purposes of subsection (b)(2)(C); or

"(C) any adjustment made under subsection (c)(2);

means information that establishes the accuracy of such amount, difference, or adjustment."

carriers certificate

To the District Director of Customs: _____

_____
(Port of entry)

_____
(Date)

The undersigned carrier, to whom or upon whose order the articles described below or in the attached document must be

released,* hereby certifies that _____ of _____ is the owner or consignee of such articles within

the purview of section 484(h), Tariff Act of 1930.

Marks and number of packages	Description and quantity of merchandise— Number and kind of packages	Gross weight in pounds	Foreign port of landing and date of sailing	Bill of lading number

Carrier _____ _____
(Name of carrier)

Voyage No. _____

Arrived_____ _____
(Date)   (Agent)

*Under the tariff laws of the United States Customs officers do not deliver the goods to the consignee. The goods are released from Customs custody to or upon the order of the carrier by whom the goods are brought to the port at which they are entered for consumption. When the goods are entered for warehouse, they are released from Customs custody to or upon the order of the proprietor of the warehouse.

Department of the Treasury
U S Customs Service
141.32, C R.

POWER OF ATTORNEY

Check appropriate box
☐ Individual
☐ Partnership
☐ Corporation
☐ Sole Proprietorship

KNOW ALL MEN BY THESE PRESENTS That, _____
(Full Name of person, partnership, or corporation, or sole proprietorship (identify)

a corporation doing business under the laws of the State of _____ or a _____

doing business as _____ residing at _____

having an office and place of business at _____ hereby constitutes and appoints each of the following persons

_____
(Give full name of each agent designated)

as a true and lawful agent and attorney of the grantor named above for and in the name, place, and stead of said grantor from this date and in Customs District _____: and in no other name, to make, endorse, sign, declare, or swear to any entry, withdrawal, declaration, certificate, bill of lading, or other document required by law or regulation in connection with the importation, transportation, or exportation of any merchandise shipped or consigned by or to said grantor, to perform any act or condition which may be required by law or regulation in connection with such merchandise, to receive any merchandise deliverable to said grantor.

To make endorsements on bills of lading conferring authority to make entry and collect drawback, and to make, sign, declare, or swear to any statement, supplemental statement, schedule, supplemental schedule, certificate of delivery, certificate of manufacture, certificate of manufacture and delivery, abstract of manufacturing records, declaration of proprietor on drawback entry, declaration of exporter on drawback entry, or any other affidavit or document which may be required by law or regulation for drawback purposes, regardless of whether such bill of lading, sworn statement, schedule, certificate, abstract, declaration, or other affidavit or document is intended for filing in said district or in any other customs district.

To sign, seal, and deliver for and as the act of said grantor any bond required by law or regulation in connection with the entry or withdrawal of imported merchandise or merchandise exported with or without benefit of drawback, or in connection with the entry, clearance, lading, unlading or navigation of any vessel or other means of conveyance owned or operated by said grantor, and any and all bonds which may be

voluntarily given and accepted under applicable laws and regulations, consignee's and owner's declarations provided for in section 485, Tariff Act of 1930, as amended, or affidavits in connection with the entry of merchandise.

To sign and swear to any document and to perform any act that may be necessary or required by law or regulation in connection with the entering, clearing, lading, unlading, or operation of any vessel or other means of conveyance owned or operated by said grantor.

And generally to transact at the customhouses in said district any and all customs business, including making, signing, and filing of protests under section 514 of the Tariff Act of 1930, in which said grantor is or may be concerned or interested and which may properly be transacted or performed by an agent and attorney, giving to said agent and attorney full power and authority to do anything whatever requisite and necessary to be done in the premises as fully as said grantor could do if present and acting, hereby ratifying and confirming all that the said agent and attorney shall lawfully do by virtue of these presents, the foregoing power of attorney to remain in full force and effect until the _____ day of _____, 19___, or until notice of revocation in writing is duly given to and received by the District Director of Customs of the district aforesaid. If the donor of this power of attorney is a partnership, and said the power shall in no case have any force or effect after the expiration of 2 years from the date of its receipt in the office of the district director of customs of the said district.

IN WITNESS WHEREOF, the said _____

has caused these presents to be sealed and signed (Signature) _____

(Capacity) _____

WITNESS _____

(Date) _____

(Corporate seal) *(Optional)

Customs Form 5291 (10-07-80)

(SEE OVER)

INDIVIDUAL OR PARTNERSHIP CERTIFICATION *(Optional)

CITY_____
COUNTY_____ } ss:
STATE_____

On this _____ day of _____, 19____, personally appeared before me _____

residing at _____, personally known or sufficiently identified to me, who certifies that

_____ (is)(are) the individual(s) who executed the foregoing instrument and acknowledge it to be _____ free act and deed.

_____
(Notary Public)

CORPORATE CERTIFICATION *(Optional)

(To be made by an officer other than the one who executes the power of attorney)

I, _____, certify that I am the _____

of _____, organized under the laws of the State of _____

that _____, who signed this power of attorney on behalf of the donor, is the _____

of said corporation; and that said power of attorney was duly signed, sealed, and attested for and behalf of said corporation by authority of its governing body as the

same appears in a resolution of the Board of Directors passed at a regular meeting held on the _____ day of _____, now in my possession or custody. I

further certify that the resolution is in accordance with the articles of incorporation and bylaws of said corporation.

IN WITNESS WHEREOF, I have hereunto set my hand and affixed the seal of said corporation, at the City of _____ this _____ day of

_____, 19 _____

_____   _____
(Signature)   (Date)

If the corporation has no corporate seal, the fact shall be stated, in which case a scroll or adhesive shall appear in the appropriate, designated place.

Customs powers of attorney of residents (including resident corporations) shall be without power of substitution except for the purpose of executing shipper's export declarations. However, a power of attorney executed in favor of a licensed customhouse broker may specify that the power of attorney is granted to the customhouse broker to act through any of its licensed officers or any employee specifically authorized to act for such customhouse broker by power of attorney.

*NOTE: The corporate seal may be omitted. Customs does not require completion of a certification. The grantor has the option of executing the certification or omitting it.

Note: Side two of CF5291, Power of Attorney, is optional. It is included here for the reader's clarification.

Approved through 4/30/87 OMB No. 1515-0144

| 1. THIS FORM MUST BE TYPED.
2. DO NOT ALTER THIS FORM.
3. ORIGINAL TO BE SUBMITTED TO CUSTOMS. (See Option explained in Instruction no. 2.) | DEPARTMENT OF THE TREASURY
UNITED STATES CUSTOMS SERVICE
CORPORATE SURETY POWER OF ATTORNEY | CUSTOMS USE ONLY
DATE RECEIVED

EFFECTIVE DATE |

☐ GRANT (Instruction No. 3a.)   ☐ CHANGE to Grant on file (Instruction No. 3b.)   ☐ REVOCATION. The below-described powers previously granted are hereby revoked. (Instruction No. 3c.)

GRANTEE:

NAME _____ ☐ This is a name change   ADDRESS _____ ☐ This is an address change.

SOCIAL SECURITY NO. _____

GRANTOR:

Surety Company's Corporate Name _____ | Surety No. | State Under Whose laws organized as a surety

District Code(s) for Customs district(s) in which authorized to do business and limit on any single obligation -OR- district(s) being added to the original grant:

District	Limit	District	Limit	District	Limit	District	Limit	District	Limit	District	Limit

Grantor appoints the above-named person (Grantee) as its attorney in fact to sign its name as surety to, and to execute, seal, and acknowledge any bond so as to bind the surety corporation to the same extent as if done by a regularly elected officer, limited only to the extent shown above as to Customs district and amount on any single bond obligation. This grant, or change to a grant on file, or revocation, as specified, shall become active on the effective date shown provided the Customs Form 5297 is received at a district office 5 days before the effective date shown; otherwise the specified action will become active at the close of business 5 working days after the date of receipt at the district office.

| In witness whereof, the said Grantor, by virtue of authority conferred by its Board of Directors, has caused these presents to be sealed with its corporate seal and attested by any two principal officers. | Date Attested

Use a facsimile of corporate seal, and not impression seal. | Name and Title

SIGNATURE: | Name and Title

SIGNATURE: |

CUSTOMS FORM 5297 (113082)

Approved through 01/31/91
OMB No. 1515-0144

DEPARTMENT OF THE TREASURY
UNITED STATES CUSTOMS SERVICE

CUSTOMS BOND

19 CFR Part 113

CUSTOMS USE ONLY	BOND NUMBER[1] (Assigned by Customs)
	FILE REFERENCE

In order to secure payment of any duty, tax or charge and compliance with law or regulation as a result of activity covered by any condition referenced below, we, the below named principal(s) and surety(ies), bind ourselves to the United States in the amount or amounts, as set forth below.

Execution Date

SECTION I—Select Single Transaction OR Continuous Bond (not both) and fill in the applicable blank spaces.

☐ SINGLE TRANSACTION BOND	Identification of transaction secured by this bond (e.g., entry no., seizure no., etc.)	Date of transaction	Transaction district & port code
☐ CONTINUOUS BOND	Effective date	This bond remains in force for one year beginning with the effective date and for each succeeding annual period, or until terminated. This bond constitutes a separate bond for each period in the amounts listed below for liabilities that accrue in each period. The intention to terminate this bond must be conveyed within the time period and manner prescribed in the Customs Regulations.	

SECTION II— This bond includes the following agreements.[2] (Check one box only, except that, 1a may be checked independently or with 1, and 3a may be checked independently or with 3. Line out all other parts of this section that are not used.)

Activity Code	Activity Name and Customs Regulations in which conditions codified	Limit of Liability	Activity Code	Activity Name and Customs Regulations in which conditions codified	Limit of Liability
☐ 1	Importer or broker....................113.62		☐ 5	Public Gauger.........................113.67	
☐ 1a	Drawback Payment Refunds.............113.65		☐ 6	Wool & Fur Products Labeling Acts Importation (Single Entry Only)........113.68	
☐ 2	Custodian of bonded merchandise..........113.63 (Includes bonded carriers, freight forwarders, cartmen and lightermen, all classes of warehouses, container station operators)		☐ 7	Bill of Lading (Single Entry Only)........113.69	
			☐ 8	Detention of Copyrighted Material (Single Entry Only)................113.70	
☐ 3	International Carrier..................113.64		☐ 9	Neutrality (Single Entry Only).............113.71	
☐ 3a	Instruments of International Traffic.113.66		☐ 10	Court Costs for Condemned Goods (Single Entry Only)................113.72	
☐ 4	Foreign Trade Zone Operator.................113.73				

SECTION III— List below all tradenames or unincorporated divisions that will be permitted to obligate this bond in the principal's name including their Customs Identification Number(s).[3] (If more space is needed, use Section III(Continuation) on back of form.)

Importer Number	Importer Name	Importer Number	Importer Name
		Total number of importer names listed in Section III:	

Principal and surety agree that any charge against the bond under any of the listed names is as though it was made by the principal(s).

Principal and surety agree that they are bound to the same extent as if they executed a separate bond covering each set of conditions incorporated by reference to the Customs Regulations into this bond.

If the surety fails to appoint an agent under Title 6, United States Code, Section 7, surety consents to service on the Clerk of any United States District Court or the U.S. Court of International Trade, where suit is brought on this bond. That clerk is to send notice of the service to the surety at:

Mailing Address Requested by the Surety

	Name and Address	Importer No.[3]	
PRINCIPAL[4]		SIGNATURE[5]	SEAL
PRINCIPAL[4]	Name and Address	Importer No.[3]	
		SIGNATURE[5]	SEAL
SURETY[4,6]	Name and Address[6]	Surety No.[7]	
		SIGNATURE[5]	SEAL
SURETY[4,6]	Name and Address[6]	Surety No.[7]	
		SIGNATURE[5]	SEAL
SURETY AGENTS	Name[8]	Identification No.[9] Name[8]	Identification No.[9]

PART 1—U.S. CUSTOMS

Customs Form 301 (092189)

SECTION III (Continuation)

Importer Number	Importer Name	Importer Number	Importer Name

WITNESSES	SIGNED, SEALED, and DELIVERED in the PRESENCE OF:	
Two witnesses are required to authenticate the signature of any person who signs as an individual or as a partner; however, a witness may authenticate the signatures of both such non-corporate principals and sureties. No witness is needed to authenticate the signature of a corporate official or agent who signs for the corporation.	Name and Address of Witness for the Principal	Name and Address of Witness for the Surety
	SIGNATURE:	SIGNATURE:
	Name and Address of Witness for the Principal	Name and Address of Witness for the Surety
	SIGNATURE:	SIGNATURE:

EXPLANATIONS AND FOOTNOTES

1. The Customs Bond Number is a control number assigned by Customs to the bond contract when the bond is approved by an authorized Customs official.
2. For all bond coverage available and the language of the bond conditions refer to Part 113, subpart G, Customs Regulations.
3. The Importer Number is the Customs identification number filed pursuant to section 24.5, Customs Regulations. When the Internal Revenue Service employer identification number is used the two-digit suffix code must be shown.
4. If the principal or surety is a corporation, the name of the State in which incorporated must be shown.
5. See witness requirement above.

6. Surety Name, if a corporation, shall be the company's name as it is spelled in the Surety Companies Annual List published in the Federal Register by the Department of the Treasury (Treasury Department Circular 570).
7. Surety Number is the three digit identification code assigned by Customs to a surety company at the time the surety company initially gives notice to Customs that the company will be writing Customs bonds.
8. Surety Agent is the individual granted a Corporate Surety Power of Attorney, CF 5297, by the surety company executing the bond.
9. Agent Identification No. shall be the individual's Social Security number as shown on the Corporate Surety Power of Attorney, CF 5297, filed by the surety granting such power of attorney.

Customs Form 301 (092189) (Back)

ENTRY SUMMARY

Form Approved OMB No. 1515-0065

1. Entry No.	2. Entry Type Code	3. Entry Summary Date
4. Entry Date	5. Port Code	
6. Bond No.	7. Bond Type Code	8. Broker/Importer File No.

9. Ulimate Consignee Name and Address	10. Consignee No.	11. Importer of Record Name and Address	12. Importer No.

		13. Exporting Country	14. Export Date
		15. Country of Origin	16. Missing Documents
	State	17. I.T. No.	18. I.T. Date

19. B/L or AWB No.	20. Mode of Transportation	21. Manufacturer I.D.	22. Reference No.
23. Importing Carrier	24. Foreign Port of Lading	25. Location of Goods/G.O. No.	
26. U.S. Port of Unlading	27. Import Date		

28. Line No.	30. A. T.S.U.S.A. No. / B. ADA/CVD Case No.	29. Description of Merchandise	31. A. Gross Weight / B. Manifest Qty.	32. Net Quantity in T.S.U.S.A. Units	33. A. Entered Value / B. CHGS / C. Relationship	34. A. T.S.U.S.A. Rate / B. ADA/CVD Rate / C. I.R.C. Rate / D. Visa No.	35. Duty and I.R. Tax Dollars	Cents

36. Declaration of Importer of Record (Owner or Purchaser) or Authorized Agent

I declare that I am the
☐ importer of record and that the actual owner, purchaser, or consignee for customs purposes is as shown above.

OR

☐ owner or purchaser or agent thereof.

I further declare that the merchandise
☐ was obtained pursuant to a purchase or agreement to purchase and that the prices set forth in the invoice are true.

OR

☐ was not obtained pursuant to a purchase or agreement to purchase and the statements in the invoice as to value or price are true to the best of my knowledge and belief.

I also declare that the statements in the documents herein filed fully disclose to the best of my knowledge and belief the true prices, values, quantities, rebates, drawbacks, fees, commissions, and royalties and are true and correct, and that all goods or services provided to the seller of the merchandise either free or at reduced cost are fully disclosed. I will immediately furnish to the appropriate customs officer any information showing a different state of facts.

Notice required by Paperwork Reduction Act of 1980: This information is needed to ensure that importers/exporters are complying with U.S. customs laws, to allow us to compute and collect the right amount of money, to enforce other agency requirements, and to collect accurate statistical information on imports. Your response is mandatory. (Continued on back of form.)

↓ U.S. CUSTOMS USE ↓		TOTALS	
A. Liq. Code	B. Ascertained Duty	37. Duty	
	C. Ascertained Tax	38. Tax	
	D. Ascertained Other	39. Other	
	E. Ascertained Total	40. Total	

41. Signature of Declarant, Title, and Date

Customs Form 7501 (081790)

★ U.S. GOVERNMENT PRINTING OFFICE: 1992 - 343 - 037/74953